If we take care of the moments, the years will take care of themselves.

The classic treasury of

CHILDHOOD WONDERS

Favorite adventures,
stories, poems,
and songs for
making lasting memories

Susan H. Magsamen

NATIONAL GEOGRAPHIC

Washington, D.C.

TABLE OF CONTENTS

Wonderful adventures await...

It's all here—songs, nursery rhymes, stories, beautiful art, and activities. I hope that many of these adventures will become part of the memories you and the children in your life make together. *The Classic Treasury of Childhood Wonders* is filled with the things that many of us who made this book did as kids or wanted to do!

Play is a child's world and it's how he or she learns. How children play is, in many ways, who they will become. So encouraging kids to play frees them to develop into confident, competent, happy adults. There are over 30 adventures and activities throughout this book from outdoor explorations to arts and crafts, from kitchen chemistry to bedtime stories.

All the activities can be completed independently by a five-year-old child, unless recommended otherwise. Younger children may need help from an adult. *Childhood Wonders* can be opened on any page, anytime, for instant adventure. Take your time and be sure to have fun! Any time and place can be perfect to begin an activity.

These activities have been evaluated based on the 6 Cs™. This simple skill-based learning assessment identifies six skills essential for the 21st century global world. They are Collaboration, Communication, Content, Critical thinking, Creative innovation, and Confidence. Every activity is coded with symbols representing the C skills the activity reinforces. See the skills section on page 132 to learn more about the 6 Cs™.

Time goes by so fast, and while we think we will have time to do all the things we want with our children, the reality is, in a flash they are grown. Take the time now to play, laugh, make silly faces, and enjoy all of the moments that really do matter. Fill your children's lives with the time and adventures and love they need to grow strong and happy.

So, come and sit down. Find a comfy chair, a soft blanket and a willing, eager child. See the world through the child's eyes. Kiss and hug your little ones and tell them every day how much they are loved. *Childhood Wonders* is filled with magical explorations and hours of fun, sure to create memories that your children will cherish and enjoy for a lifetime.

Susan Magsamen

◄ *ATTIC SCENE*
BY JAMES M. GURNEY

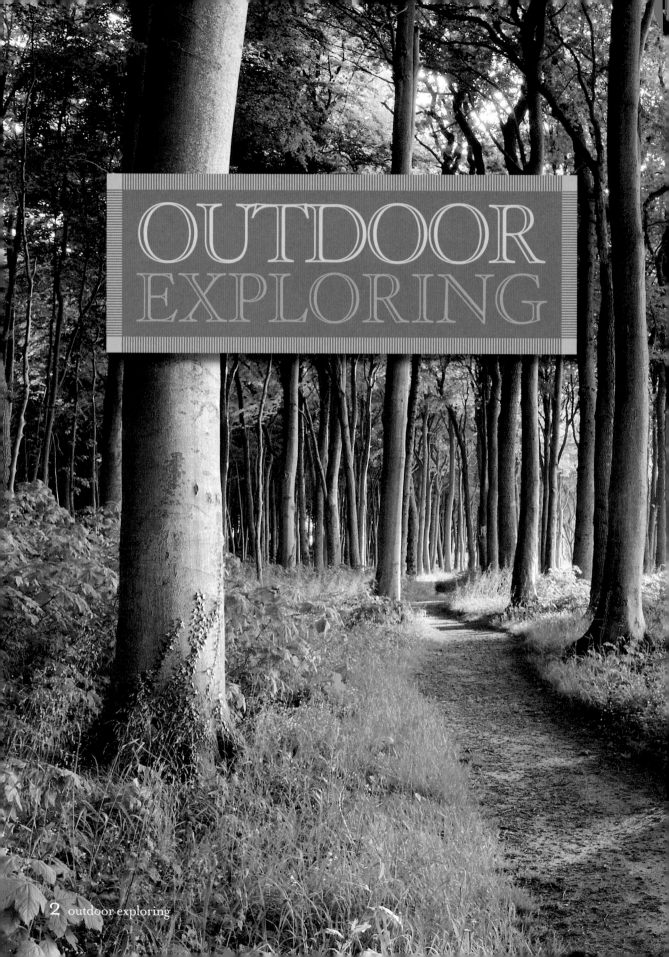

OUTDOOR EXPLORING

Follow the path to wondrous adventures...

IN THE GARDEN

The Flowers

All the names I know from nurse:
Gardener's garters,
Shepherd's purse,
Bachelor's buttons, Lady's smock,
And the Lady Hollyhock.
Fairy places, fairy things,
Fairy woods where the wild
    bee wings,
Tiny trees for tiny dames—
These must all be fairy names!
Tiny woods below whose boughs
Shady fairies weave a house;
Tiny treetops, rose or thyme,
Where the braver fairies climb!
Fair are grown-up people's trees,
But the fairest woods are these;
Where, if I were not so tall,
I should live for good and all.

ROBERT LOUIS STEVENSON

Mary, Mary

Mary, Mary, quite contrary
How does your garden grow?
With silver bells and cockle shells
And pretty maids all in a row.

NURSERY RHYME

The Rose is Red

The rose is red,
The violet's blue;
Sugar is sweet,
And so are you!

NURSERY RHYME

"The flowers that sleep by night, opened their gentle eyes and turned them to the day. The light, creation's mind, was everywhere, and all things owned its power."

CHARLES DICKENS

◀ *CARNATION, LILY, LILY, ROSE*
BY JOHN SINGER SARGENT

IN THE GARDEN
PLANT A SEED

Just about everything that grows in the ground—from plants, to fruits and vegetables, to the tallest tree—begins with a seed. Some are easy to spot like those in an apple or orange or sunflower. Others you might not ever see, like those from grass or weeds.

Seeds are one of the most amazing creations of nature. And they start out as something very small. But put seeds underground, add a little water, sunlight and fresh air, and something magical happens. Out of the tiny seed come roots that stretch deep into the ground, soaking up the soil and water to create stems that rise from the ground and grow and grow and grow.

It is fun to watch how it happens. But you have to be patient, because it takes a little while for things to get started.

If you plant fig or orange seeds, you will be an adult before your seeds are trees. But in this case, patience pays off. Eventually, they will grow to be much taller than you are!

Plant a Special Garden

WHAT YOU NEED:

- SEEDS FOR
  - SUNFLOWERS
  - LETTUCE
  - RADISHES
  - SNOW PEAS
  - CHERRY TOMATOES
  - NASTURTIUMS
  - BUSH BEANS
- CONTAINER WITH SOIL
- WATERING CAN
- GARDEN TOOLS —HAND TROWEL
- STICKS AND STRING

SKILLS:

COLLABORATION   COMMUNICATION

CONTENT

1. Fill a large container with soil. Terra cotta pots are perfect; they have holes in the bottom and a saucer to capture water. Make a sign that says "My Garden."

2. Prepare the soil by stirring it, taking out rocks and other large items.

3. Follow the instructions on the seed packet to plant your seeds. Plant a combination of seeds, such as lettuce and nasturtiums. Sunflowers, bush beans, and cherry tomatoes will need to be staked and need lots of room.

4. Remember to water your seeds as instructed and watch them grow. Most seeds sprout within days!

5. Continue to tend to your plants, watering them until they are ready to harvest. The lettuce will be first. Why not make a great salad!

SNOW, SNOW, SNOW

Beautiful Snow

Oh! The snow, the beautiful snow,
Filling the sky and the earth below;
Over the house-tops, over the street,
Over the heads of the people you meet;
Dancing, flirting, skimming along.

Beautiful snow! It can do
    nothing wrong.
Flying to kiss a fair lady's cheek;
Clinging to lips in a frolicsome freak.
Beautiful snow, from the heavens above,
Pure as an angel and fickle as love!

Oh! The snow, the beautiful snow!
How the flakes gather and laugh
    as they go!
Whirling about in its maddening fun,
It plays in its glee with everyone.
Chasing, laughing, hurrying by.

It lights up the face and it sparkles
    the eyes;
And even the dogs, with a bark
    and a bound,
Snap at the crystals that eddy around.
The town is alive, and its heart in a glow
To welcome the coming of
    beautiful snow.

JOHN W. WATSON

"Nature chose for a tool, not the earthquake or lightning to rend and split asunder, not the stormy torrent or eroding rain, but the tender snow-flowers noiselessly falling through unnumbered centuries."

JOHN MUIR

"Where does the white go when the snow melts?"

AUTHOR UNKNOWN

◀ *SNOWBALL FIGHT*
BY RUDOLF BERGANDER

SNOW, SNOW, SNOW
GO OUT & PLAY

Where did all the color go? The world changes to white with snow.

Snow is tiny ice crystals that form in the sky when the temperature is near freezing. When those ice crystals gather together, they form snow-flakes. It's said that no two snowflakes are the same, but neither are any two creations made from snow!

Take snowballs. You can make them as small as a golf ball, as large as a softball, round or bumpy, soft or hard.

No two snowmen are the same either. Ever see one with carrots for noses or buttons for eyes? Some have old jackets, tall hats, even shoes.

Then there are snow angels. Lie on your back in the snow and wave your arms and legs. Stand up carefully and look at the marks you made in the snow. It's a snow angel!

There are so many other things to do in the snow, like making ice sculptures and snow forts. What about snow families, snow cones with chocolate sauce, snow boarding and sledding? How about cross-country and downhill skiing? And don't forget to simply catch a snowflake on your tongue!

Make a Snow Family

WHAT YOU NEED:

- SNOW
- PEBBLES
- BUTTONS
- CARROTS
- OLD SCARVES
- STICKS AND TWIGS
- WARM CLOTHES

SKILLS:

COLLABORATION

CRITICAL THINKING

COMMUNICATION

CREATIVE INNOVATION

If it is snowing you know what to do! Bundle up and head outside to play. Wet snow is the best snow for making a snow family. Find some friends to build it with you.

1. To begin, scoop some snow in your hands and make a small ball. Pack it firmly.

2. Roll the ball over the snow on the ground. It will begin to pick up the snow on the ground.

small ▭▭▭▭▶ BIG

3. The snowball will get larger and larger. Keep packing it tightly. When the sun comes out your snow person will not melt as fast!

4. Make three snowballs of different sizes. One each for the bottom, middle and top — which will become the head.

5. Pile your snowballs to make a snowperson.

BOTTOM   MIDDLE   TOP

6. Now you are ready to decorate. Use a carrot for a nose, or maybe stones for the mouth and eyes. What about a hat and scarf? Be creative!

7. Make a snowperson for everyone in your family! What about the dog?

8. Take a picture of your snow family. It won't last forever.

Want More Fun?
Try making snow ice cream. It is simple: Add 2 cups (473 ml) milk, 2 cups (473 ml) sugar and a little vanilla to a 2-quart (1.8 l) bowl of fresh snow. What a "cool" treat.

A SECRET PLACE

Secret Garden

Fresh morning dew, still
dripping from the rose,
the blue birds sing their
wishful, songs of hopes.
My garden has still breath—it alone knows,
the secrets that are bound with grassy ropes.
Pure love is endless—the bird's
sing of truth,
sweet blossoms bow so humbly,
to their voice.
They rest in old age and then
dance in youth,
blameless and pure of heart—they all rejoice.
They're out of sight—hidden—
like precious gems,
the rainbows do yield, while all
time transcends.
The roses stand tall on their thorny stems,
as giving thanks, to their fair
feathered friends.
My secret garden cast
your spell in mist.
Mark down your truths
on an unending list.

WILLIAM SHAKESPEARE

Tree Fort

I saw their cabin
a-building in these woods
with one sentry high
upon the wooden heights,
familiar shouts from
neighbour-children
measuring and pounding
and growing tall
amid life's rush of noise,
a secret spot to
fill their souls, time
for special friends
they say…
a fun place, with lots of space.

RICHARD L. PROVENCHER

"What lies behind us
and what lies before us
are tiny matters
compared to what
lies within us."

RALPH WALDO EMERSON

◀ *TREE CLIMBING*
BY NOMEKO

A SECRET PLACE
FORTS & HIDEOUTS

Have you ever played a game where you found treasure and had to hide the goodies from pirates? Did you hide from those evil pirates, too? Weren't you glad to have a secret hiding place?

There are some really famous secret places. Pirates like Blackbeard hid their treasures in caves. English castles have secret chambers and passages for quick escapes. Authors have special places to write and artists have special places for painting. Wildlife photographers also have secret places to hide to photograph animals. Some wonderful books that take us to imaginary secret places include *The Chronicles of Narnia* series, *Alice in Wonderland*, *The Secret Garden*, *The Harry Potter* series, and *Robinson Crusoe*.

Everyone can have a secret hiding place, a fort or a hideout. It might be a place indoors where no one would think to look for you, like behind the sofa in your living room, underneath the dining room table, or between huge footlockers or boxes in the attic.

An outdoor secret hiding place is a great place to watch the world go by. In the yard or woods you can make forts and hideouts, from everything from old tree stumps to tall rocks.

Just make sure that your hiding place isn't a secret to grown-ups. And don't forget to invite friends to visit you from time to time.

Make a Hideout

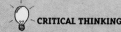

WHAT YOU NEED:

- BLANKETS, SHEETS, BEACH TOWELS
- CARDBOARD BOXES • FLASHLIGHT
- PILLOWS • SNACKS • BOOKS FOR READING AND FOR WEIGHT
- PAPER AND MARKERS
- CD PLAYER, iPOD

SKILLS:

CRITICAL THINKING   CREATIVE INNOVATION

There are lots of ways to make a secret place inside and outside. Here are some ideas for making both!

Inside Hideout Ideas

1. The place under the dining room or kitchen table is perfect. So is a basement or attic. Another great place is under your bed or in your closet. Search around and find a perfect location for your hideout.

2. Grab some blankets, sheets or beach towels.

3. Drape the blankets over a table or chairs to create a "tent" roof and walls. Secure them with heavy books. Make a door to get in and out of.

4. Bring inside all the stuff you need. You might want a flashlight, snacks, a soft pillow, books, paper, markers, and music.

5. Let the time fly. Maybe even invite a friend for a visit.

Want More Fun? Build a Hideout Outside!

Forts can be built out of all kinds of things like cardboard boxes, logs, sticks, piles of leaves—you name it.

1. Scope out the perfect place. What about in a tree, under a bush, behind a shed or garage?

2. Think about how you will build it and begin to make your hideout. What about making a window to the sky for stargazing?

3. Put your supplies inside. A sleeping bag is a nice addition for this home away from home.

Climb inside and enjoy. Don't forget to tell your folks where you are!

SALT, SEA & SAND

The Castle Builder

A gentle boy, with soft and silken locks
A dreamy boy, with brown and tender eyes,
A castle-builder, with his wooden blocks,
And towers that touch imaginary skies.

A fearless rider on his father's knee,
An eager listener unto stories told
At the Round Table of the nursery,
Of heroes and adventures manifold.

There will be other towers for thee to build;
There will be other steeds for thee to ride;
There will be other legends, and all filled
With greater marvels and more glorified.

Build on, and make thy castles high and fair,
Rising and reaching upward to the skies;
Listen to voices in the upper air,
Nor lose thy simple faith in mysteries.

HENRY WADSWORTH LONGFELLOW

She Sells Seashells

She sells seashells by the seashore.
The shells she sells are seashells.
I'm sure for if she sells shells
on the seashore,
I'm sure she sells seashore shells.

TERRY SULLIVAN

"Build castles
in the air."

ROBERT BURTON

"To see a world in a grain of sand, and a heaven
in a wild flower, hold infinity in the palm of
your hands, and eternity in an hour."

WILLIAM BLAKE

◀ *RING AROUND THE ROSY (DETAIL)*
BY EDWARD HENRY POTTHAST

SALT, SEA & SAND
MAGIC CASTLES & SEASHELLS

For every sand-filled beach there are thousands of seashells waiting to be collected and hundreds of sand castles waiting to be built. Seashells and sand castles are what make any trip to the beach fun.

Seashells protect animals—many of which don't have skeletons—from other animals that could harm them.

Seashells come in all sorts of sizes, shapes, and colors. Some are spiral, while others are like saucers. The fun thing about some seashells, such as conchs, is that if you put them up to your ear you can hear a sound that's like the ocean. Give it a try the next time you are at the beach.

Like snowflakes, no two sand castles are the same.

The world's largest sand castle was recorded in 2007 at 31 feet, 6 inches (9.4 m, 15 cm) tall, built by Ed Jarrett at Point Sebago in Casco, Maine. Sand castles don't have to be big to be really fun to make!

Make a Sand Castle

WHAT YOU NEED:

- SHOVELS • SHELLS, STICKS, DRIFTWOOD, SEA GLASS, AND STONES
- STRING • VARIOUS-SIZE BUCKETS
- SAND • WATER

SKILLS:

COLLABORATION

COMMUNICATION

CONTENT

CRITICAL THINKING

CREATIVE INNOVATION

1. Scoop wet sand onto the center of the area where you'll be working to make your foundation.

2. Sand castles have two major parts—towers and walls. To build towers pack your bucket with sand. Carefully turn the bucket upside down and pull off. Use different size buckets to make a range of towers.

3. The towers will become the anchors for the walls. To construct walls to connect the towers of your castle create brick shapes with wet sand and lay them on top of one another.

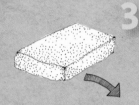

4. Carve windows, doors, and details in your sand castle using a twig or plastic knife.

5. Arches, ramps, and stairs can also be added. Build stairs going around the towers by creating narrow ramps and carving in steps.

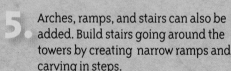
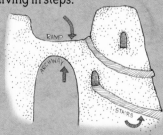

6. Add shells for shingles and pebbles for doorknobs. Sea glass also makes beautiful decorations. Small pieces of driftwood make great little soldiers. Put a flag to fly on the top of the castle, too.

7. Use the dribble technique to create a cool effect. To do this you need very wet sand. Hold it in your fingers and let it slowly "dribble" out between your fingers and hands.

8. Many castles have moats to protect them from invaders—like waves, dogs, and other kids!

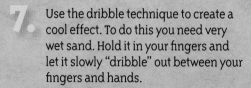

Be sure to take a picture of your sand castle before it washes away.

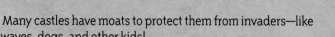

RUN AND PLAY

Jupiter and the Monkey

Jupiter issued a proclamation to all the beasts of the forest and promised a royal reward to the one whose offspring should be deemed the handsomest. The Monkey came with the rest and presented, with all a mother's tenderness, a flat-nosed, hairless, ill-featured young Monkey as a candidate for the promised reward. A general laugh saluted her on the presentation of her son. She resolutely said, "I know not whether Jupiter will allot the prize to my son, but this I do know, that he is at least in the eyes of me his mother, the dearest, handsomest, and most beautiful of all.

AESOP FABLE

Ten Little Monkeys

Ten little monkeys jumping
    on the bed,
One fell off and bumped
    his head;
Momma called the doctor,
    the doctor said,
"No more monkeys jumping
on the bed!"

Repeat counting down till…

One little monkey jumping
    on the bed,
He fell out and bumped
    his head;
Momma called the doctor,
    the doctor said,
"No more monkeys jumping
on the bed!"

No little monkeys jumping
    on the bed,
None fell off and bumped
    their heads;
Momma called the doctor,
    the doctor said,
"Put those monkeys straight
    back to bed."

CHILDREN'S SONG

◀ *LITTLE MONKEY*
BY SANDRA MAGSAMEN

RUN AND PLAY
HOP, SKIP & JUMP

How fast can you run? How high can you jump? Can you touch a leaf on a branch above you? How far can you skip? It's fine to play video or computer games, but nothing beats the fun you have with running, jumping, and skipping.

Once Marla Runyan, a woman who ran long distances in the Olympics, was asked, "When did you start running?" She replied, "When did you stop?" Because running is what most of us do almost as soon as we learn to walk. We can't wait to take off to see how fast we can go.

The same thing goes for hopping. It's fun to see how high you can hop. Stand beside a wall and raise your arm straight above you. Have a grown-up mark on the wall where your fingertips touch. That's as high as you can reach.

Then, at that same spot, jump as high as you can and touch the wall, then have the grown-up mark that spot. That's as high as you can jump. As you get older, see how much distance you can get between your reach and your jump.

Skipping games are fun to play outdoors, especially with a friend. Some of your favorite songs can be even more fun when sung to a skip. And best of all, running, jumping and skipping are good exercise, which means they keep you fit.

Some Fun Ways to Move

WHAT YOU NEED:
YOU AND
YOUR FRIENDS!

SKILLS:
COLLABORATION

CONTENT

COMMUNICATION

1. Hopping
How many times can you hop on one foot? Count and see.

1,2,3...

2. Skipping
Have you ever tried skipping? It's an alternate knee-up step with a hop. See how far you can go. Skipping makes you happy!

3. Spinning
Close your eyes and spin around in a circle 10 times. Now stop. Is the world still spinning?

4. Dancing
Turn on your favorite music as loud as you can and dance, dance, dance. It feels great!

5. Running
Try running just for fun. Run as far as you can. Feel the wind on your face.

ENCHANTED NIGHTS

The Moon

The moon has a face like
    the clock in the hall;
She shines on thieves on
    the garden wall,
On streets and fields and
    harbor quays,
And birdies asleep in the forks
    of the trees.

The squalling cat and the
    squeaking mouse,
The howling dog by the
    door of the house,
The bat that lies in bed at noon,
All love to be out by the light
    of the moon.

But all of the things that
    belong to the day
Cuddle to sleep to be
    out of her way;
And flowers and children
    close their eyes
Till up in the morning the
    sun shall rise.

ROBERT LOUIS STEVENSON

"How sweet the
moonlight sleeps
upon this bank.
Here will we sit,
and let the sounds
of music
Creep in our ears;
soft stillness, and
the night
Become the touches
of sweet harmony."

WILLIAM SHAKESPEARE

Poem

'Tis moonlight, summer moonlight,
This moonlight, summer moonlight,
All soft and still and fair;
The solemn hour of midnight
Breathes sweet thoughts everywhere.

EMILY JANE BRONTË

◀ *MOTHER AND CHILD AT NIGHT*
UNKNOWN ARTIST

ENCHANTED NIGHTS
LIGHT UP THE SKY

During the summertime, nature gives us all sorts of things that help light up the night. There's the glow of the moon, the twinkling of stars, lightning from storms, and then there are lightning bugs.

They're better known as fireflies, although they're really not flies at all. Did you know that firefly, lightning bug, and glow worm are all names for the same insect? But this insect is not a worm or a fly. It's a beetle, and it flies for only a short time. These beetles are known for the light in their tails, a bright yellow glow that goes on and off as they fly.

A firefly can make light whenever it wants, and each firefly species has its own unique code. The fireflies use the flashes of light to recognize members of their own species and to find mates. Most of the time it's the male firefly that flies around making light signals while the female stays near the ground.

Chasing fireflies will take you on a merry adventure and put a sparkle in your eye!

Make a Firefly House

WHAT YOU NEED:
- PLASTIC JAR WITH LID
- POINTED TOOL
- GRASS

SKILLS:
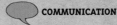

COLLABORATION

CONTENT

COMMUNICATION

1. Find a plastic mayonnaise or other jar with a lid. Wash it with soapy water and rinse well.

2. Using a pointed tool, carefully punch several holes, no larger than a toothpick, in the top of the lid. Ask your parents to help.

3. Put a couple of handfuls of grass in the bottom of the jar.

4. Once it is dark you are ready to catch a firefly. Let your eyes adjust to the night and look for blinking flashes of light.

5. Walk very quietly toward the flashes. Gently cup your hands around a firefly.

6. Carefully put the firefly in your make-shift home and screw on the lid. See how many fireflies you can catch in one night!

7. Bring the jar in the house and look closely at your fireflies. Aren't they amazing?

Before you go to bed, release all of the fireflies into the night.

WIND AT MY BACK

The Wind

I saw you toss the kites on high
And blow the birds about the sky;
And all around I heard you pass,
Like ladies' skirts across the grass—
O wind, a-blowing all day long,
O wind, that sings so loud a song!
I saw the different things you did,
But always you yourself you hid.
I felt you push, I heard you call,
I could not see yourself at all—
O wind, a-blowing all day long,
O wind, that sings so loud a song!

O you that are so strong and cold,
O blower, are you young or old?
Are you a beast of field and tree,
Or just a stronger child than me?
O wind, a-blowing all day long,
O wind, that sings so loud a song!

ROBERT LOUIS STEVENSON

The North Wind and the Sun

The North Wind and the Sun disputed as to which was the most powerful, and agreed that he should be declared the victor who could first strip a wayfaring man of his clothes. The North Wind first tried his power and blew with all his might, but the keener his blasts, the closer the Traveler wrapped his cloak around him, until at last, resigning all hope of victory, the Wind called upon the Sun to see what he could do. The Sun suddenly shone out with all his warmth. The Traveler no sooner felt his genial rays than he took off one garment after another, and at last, fairly overcome with heat, undressed and bathed in a stream that lay in his path. Persuasion is better than Force.

AESOP FABLE

"A light wind swept over the corn, and all nature laughed in the sunshine."

ANN BRONTË

WIND AT MY BACK
INTO THE AIR

Wind is one of nature's most amazing, mostly silent tools. Did you know that a combination of the heat from the sun and the rotation of the Earth causes air to move, creating wind? Wind is great for flying kites and paper airplanes. Wind chimes and whirligigs are also fun to make and take outside for the wind to whirl through.

Imagine making a small piece of paper stay in the air for nearly half a minute. That's what Ken Blackburn did with a paper airplane. In 1998, he folded his paper into the shape of a plane, hurled it into the air and watched as it stayed afloat for 27.6 seconds. His record stood for 13 years. It is a combination of wind and mechanics that makes this possible.

That's why kids aren't the only ones who enjoy making paper planes. Even airplane builders study what makes them stay in the air for so long, and they use what they learn in making real planes.

There is no one way to fold paper into a plane, as long as your plane has wings and a place to hold the plane in your fingertips—usually beneath the plane, and held between your thumb and index finger—for the throw.

The Arrow is the most famous paper airplane design. Try making one now!

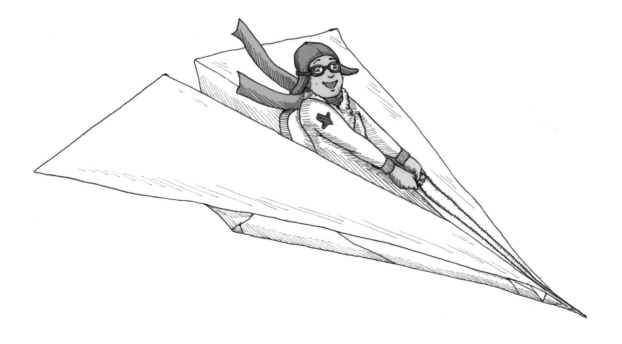

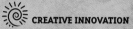

Make a Paper Airplane

SKILLS:

 CONTENT

CREATIVE INNOVATION

 CRITICAL THINKING

1. Fold a piece of paper in half long-ways. Re-open so you can see the crease between the two halves.

2. Fold each corner at one end of the paper towards the center crease.

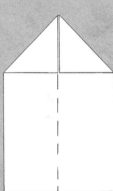

3. Beginning at the point, fold each side of the paper down till the inside edges line up with the center crease.

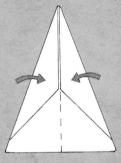

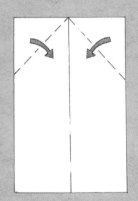

4. Fold airplane in half along center line.

5. Now, fold the first wing down, keeping the fold parallel to the centerline of the plane. This fold should be between ½ and 1 inch (1.3 and 2.5 cm) from the center. Turn the plane over, and fold the other wing the same way.

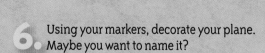

6. Using your markers, decorate your plane. Maybe you want to name it?

7. Open the wings, and make a test run. You might have to fine tune your plane for maximum speed and direction.

WANDERING & WONDERING

The Road Not Taken

Two roads diverged in a yellow wood,
And sorry I could not travel both
And be one traveler, long I stood
And looked down one as far as I could
To where it bent in the undergrowth;
Then took the other, as just as fair,
And having perhaps the better claim,
Because it was grassy and wanted wear;
Though as for that the passing there
Had worn them really about the same,
And both that morning equally lay
In leaves no step had trodden black.
Oh, I kept the first for another day!
Yet knowing how way leads on to way,
I doubted if I should ever come back.
I shall be telling this with a sigh
Somewhere ages and ages hence:
Two roads diverged in a wood, and I
I took the one less traveled by,
And that has made all the difference.

ROBERT FROST

Take the Back Roads

Take the back roads.
It takes more time
But it is worth it.
Look in the dark corners.
That's where you will find
The most interesting things
and people.
And don't be afraid
To sing your song
Even if no one else likes it
Because it is your song.

BEN GARRETT

"Wandering re-establishes the original harmony which once existed between man and the universe."

ANATOLE FRANCE

◀ *SECRET ZOO*
BY CHRIS SHEBAN

WANDERING & WONDERING
THINK CURIOUSLY

To wander is to go from one place to another with no destination planned. To wonder is to think curiously about your surroundings. A wonder is also something odd, unique, or fascinating.

Both wondering and wandering give us a chance for discovery. The difference is that one—wandering—requires that you move, while you can wonder standing still.

A good place to wonder and wander is along a hiking trail. You can wander for miles and see all the wonders of nature, from insects to plants to animals. You can do the same at the beach or at a park or in an art museum. Take a notebook and jot down things that you find interesting.

Wondering is a great thing to do almost anytime and anywhere. All you need is a curious mind and some time.

Remember to take a friend or your parents with you when you wander, and always tell an adult where you are going.

Ideas for the Nateure Wanderer

WHAT YOU NEED:
- IMAGINATION
- CURIOSITY
- NOTEBOOK AND PEN

SKILLS:

 COMMUNICATION   CREATIVE INNOVATION

 CONTENT   CONFIDENCE

CRITICAL THINKING

1. Look at a local map and find a good place. Be sure to bring an adult with you.

2. Use your senses to discover and explore things you have never seen before or see things in a new way.

Smell What do you smell? If it is fall, maybe leaves and dirt. If it is spring, maybe the flowers.

Hearing Are there birds singing? Do you hear people talking? What about the sound of the wind?

Seeing Observe what is happening around you. Is a bird making a nest? What are the colors of nature?

Touch How many different textures can you feel? How does the air feel on your face?

Keep a journal about your adventures. Wandering is about being surprised! You never know what you will find as you wander. But for sure there is always something new to discover.

PLAY BALL!

Take Me Out to the Ball Game

Katie Casey was baseball mad,
Had a fever and had it bad.
Just to root for the home town crew,
Ev'ry sou
Katie blew.
On a Saturday her young beau
Called to see if she'd like to go
To see a show, but Miss Kate said
"No, I'll tell you what you can do."

Chorus:
Take me out to the ball game,
Take me out with the crowd;
Buy me some peanuts
   and Cracker Jacks,
I don't care if I never get back.
Let me root, root, root for
   the home team,

If they don't win, it's a shame.
For it's one, two, three strikes,
   you're out,
At the old ball game.

Katie Casey saw all the games,
Knew the players by their
   first names.
Told the umpire he was wrong,
All along,
Good and strong.
When the score was just two to two
Katie Casey knew what to do,
Just to cheer up the boys she knew,
She made the gang sing this song:

(Repeat Chorus)

BY JACK NORWORTH AND
ALBERT VON TILZER

"You can't possibly
hit the ball if you're
thinking about all
the possible ways
you could miss."

AUTHOR UNKNOWN

"It's always too
early to quit."

NORMAN VINCENT PEALE

◀ *BASEBALL*
BY MACKY PAMINTUAN

PLAY BALL!
DRIBBLE, BOUNCE, THROW

Have you ever bounced a ball? Sure, most of us have. But have you ever dribbled one? What's the difference?

While you can bounce most rubber balls, dribbling is a specific kind of bouncing. It is what you do in the sport of basketball.

Dribbling is done with one hand. The palm of your hand must face the ground and pat the ball down. One of the easiest ways to dribble is to make the thumb, index, and middle fingers touch the ball like a claw, leaving the ring and pinky fingers free. Then pat the ball each time it bounces back to you. When you catch and hold the ball, you're not dribbling anymore.

Bouncing has no such rules. You can bounce with one hand or both. Same goes for throwing, although in basketball, a throw of the ball to another person is called a pass.

There are all types of throws. A chest throw is when you place the ball up to your chest and push it away from you with both hands. An underhanded throw is when you toss the ball with the palm of your hand facing the sky. For an overhead throw, you start with the ball over and behind your head.

Tossing a ball in any way is great fun and something you can do any time.

Ball Games to Play

WHAT YOU NEED:
- BASEBALL • FOOTBALL • KICKBALL
- GLOVE • FRIENDS • BLANKETS
OR SHEETS

SKILLS:

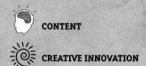

COLLABORATION

COMMUNICATION

CONTENT

CREATIVE INNOVATION

1. Step and Catch
You can use any ball for this game: Begin by standing face to face. Pass the ball back and forth. Each time a player successfully catches the ball he/she takes one step back. Keep doing this until a player drops the ball. How far can you go?

2. 500
One player is the thrower, and everyone else stands about throwing distance away from the thrower. The thrower tosses the ball in the air and calls out a number between 50 and 500. The person who catches the ball gets as many points as the thrower called out. But, if the ball is dropped the person who dropped the ball loses the same number of points. The winner is the first person to get 500 points. That person becomes the thrower and on and on.

3. Blanket Ball
Divide your group into two teams. Each team should have at least four players and a blanket. Each person on the team should hold a corner of the blanket or sheet. The game begins by having one team serve the ball by putting it in the middle of the blanket. The team lowers the blanket and quickly raises it to launch the ball. The opposite team must catch the ball in its blanket and toss it back. A point is earned for every missed pass.

4. Spud
Get together a group of kids and a large soft ball. Pick someone to be "It." "It" counts to 10 out loud. As this is happening all of the other players spread out. At 10 everyone freezes in place. Then "It" takes four giant steps toward the closest person saying "S-P-U-D" and throws the ball attempting to hit a player. If "It" hits the player, the player gets a letter "S" and becomes "It." If "It" misses the player, he/she earns the letter "S" and continues as "It." Players are eliminated once they earn "S-P-U-D." The winner is the last person standing.

Can you think of some other fun ball games?

DREAM IT MAKE IT

To create
something is to
share a little bit
of yourself.

My Shadow

I have a little shadow that goes in and out with me,
And what can be the use of him is more than I can see.
He is very, very like me from the heels up to the head;
And I see him jump before me, when I jump into my bed.
The funniest thing about him is the way he likes to grow —
Not at all like proper children, which is always very slow;
For he sometimes shoots up taller like an india-rubber ball,
And he sometimes gets so little that there's none of him at all.
He hasn't got a notion of how children ought to play,
And can only make a fool of me in every sort of way.
He stays so close beside me, he's a coward, you can see;
I'd think shame to stick to nursie as that shadow sticks to me!
One morning, very early, before the sun was up,
I rose and found the shining dew on every buttercup;
But my lazy little shadow, like an errant sleepy-head,
Had stayed at home behind me and was fast asleep in bed.

ROBERT LOUIS STEVENSON

That Shadow,
My Likeness

That shadow, my likeness, that goes to and fro,
seeking a livelihood, chattering, chaffering;
How often I find myself standing and looking at it where it flits;
How often I question and doubt whether that is really me.

WALT WHITMAN

◄ *FOOTBALLERS, KOS*
BY ANDREW MACARA

CATCHING YOUR SHADOW
SHADOW PRINTS

Imagine tracing an outline of a person's shadow on a piece of paper. That's called a silhouette; it is an image that's similar to the shadow you see on a wall when you hold up an object to light.

In the 18th century, silhouettes were created as often as paintings. A person would pose in profile, which means to turn your head to one side. The artist would then make a cutout of the person.

Most silhouettes are created on black paper placed against a white back-ground, but some are the other way around, while others are of different colors entirely. Some of the most popular silhouettes are of American Presidents, especially George Washington and Abraham Lincoln.

We see silhouettes in lots of places everyday. The NBA logo, for example, has a white silhouette of a basketball player against a red and blue background. Take a look at a road sign for a school. Inside the bright yellow sign is an image of two children walking to school. That image is a silhouette.

Make a Shadow Print

WHAT YOU NEED:
- BLACK PAPER
- EXTRA-LARGE WHITE PAPER
- A FLASHLIGHT OR DESK LAMP
- MASKING TAPE • SCISSORS • PENCIL
- CHALK • GLUE

SKILLS:
 COLLABORATION
 CONTENT
 COMMUNICATION
 CREATIVE INNOVATION

1. Tape a white piece of paper to a wall in a light-free room and arrange your subject with his/her profile in the middle of the paper.

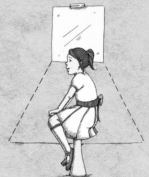

2. Turn on the flashlight or lamp. Shine the lights on your subject. You will see a shadow clearly on the white paper! Tell your subject to sit very still.

3. Trace around the subject's shadow with a pencil.

4. Carefully cut out the traced profile from the white paper.

5. Now transfer this image to black paper. Place the white cutout on the black paper and trace with a pencil or piece of chalk. Cut out the second image in black.

6. Glue the black image onto a new piece of white paper.

7. Frame your silhouette and hang it in a special place or give it as a gift.

Try creating a silhouette of your hands, too!

STORIES COME TO LIFE

The Phoenix Bird

The Bird of Paradise—renewed each century—born in flame, ending in flame! Thy picture, in a golden frame, hangs in the halls of the rich, but thou thyself often fliest around, lonely and disregarded, a myth— "The Phoenix of Arabia."

In Paradise, when thou wert born in the first rose, beneath the Tree of Knowledge, thou receivedst a kiss, and thy right name was given thee— thy name, Poetry.

HANS CHRISTIAN ANDERSEN

The Land of Counterpane

When I was sick and lay a-bed,
I had two pillows at my head,
And all my toys beside me lay,
To keep me happy all the day.

And sometimes for an hour or so
I watched my leaden soldiers go,
With different uniforms and drills,
Among the bed-clothes, through the hills;

And sometimes sent my ships in fleets
All up and down among the sheets;
Or brought my trees and houses out,
And planted cities all about.

I was the giant great and still
That sits upon the pillow-hill,
And sees before him, dale and plain,
The pleasant land of counterpane.

ROBERT LOUIS STEVENSON

◀ *PUNCH AND JUDY*
JOHN ANTHONY PULLER

STORIES COME TO LIFE
PUPPET THEATER

Puppets have been around for a long, long time—some people say for thousands of years! Puppets can be found in almost every country around the world. Asian countries are famous for their shadow puppets, Europe for beautiful wooden characters.

The people who create and make puppets move are called puppeteers. These artists craft puppets from many types of material including fabric, wood, and even paper.

You can make puppets from just about anything. Dolls, stuffed animals or objects that can be made to move are perfect. Some puppets fit over the hand; they have tiny pockets inside their bodies that you stick your fingers into to make them dance, clap, walk, jump, and do tricks. Some are so tiny that they fit over your fingers. Others move because their bodies are attached to strings, wires, or rods that you pull.

Puppet shows are a great way to tell a story or sing songs. Many famous stories have been told and retold through puppets. Folk tales, fables, myths, and legends are very popular. Sometimes an actor will play the voices for all of the characters, and other times there are several actors.

Make Some Finger Puppets

WHAT YOU NEED:

- OLD GLOVES • POMPOMS
- FELT AND FABRIC SCRAPS
- MARKERS OR PENS • GOOGLY EYES • YARN
- GLUE OR GLUE GUN • SCISSORS

SKILLS:

 COLLABORATION

CONTENT

COMMUNICATION

CREATIVE INNOVATION

Decide what story you want to tell. Maybe the "Three Little Pigs," "Cinderella," or the "Princess and the Frog"?

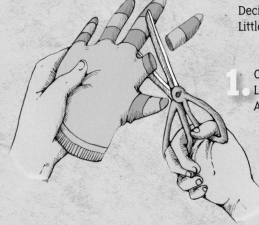

1. Carefully cut the fingers off an old pair of gloves. Lay out the finger pouches on a covered workspace. Ask an adult for help with this.

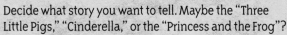

2. Design your puppet characters using googly eyes, yarn for hair, felt pieces for faces, fabric for clothes and markers for extra details.

3. Using glue or a glue gun attach pieces on the finger pouches and let dry.

4. Now you are ready to put on a puppet show. Create a stage and invite your family and friends.

Tip: Use old socks if you want to make larger puppets to fit on your hand.

HAND IN HAND

Eeny, Meeny, Miny, Moe

Eeny, Meeny, Miny, Moe,
Catch a tiger by the toe.
If he hollers let him go,
Eeny, meeny, miny, moe.
My mother told me to pick
the very best one,
And that is YOU.

ENGLISH COUNTING RHYME

This Little Piggy

This little piggy went to market,
This little piggy stayed at home,
This little piggy had roast beef,
This little piggy had none.
And this little piggy went…
"Wee wee wee" all the way home…

ACTION RHYME

One, Two, Buckle My Shoe

One, two,
Buckle my shoe;
Three, four,
Knock at the door;
Five, six,
Pick up sticks;
Seven, eight,
Lay them straight;
Nine, ten,
A big fat hen;
Eleven, twelve,
Dig and delve;
Thirteen, fourteen,
Maids a-courting;
Fifteen, sixteen,
Maids in the kitchen;
Seventeen, eighteen,
Maids a-waiting,
Nineteen, twenty,
My plate's empty

ENGLISH COUNTING RHYME

◀ *NOTHING BUT MIRACLES*
BY SUSAN L. ROTH

HAND IN HAND
GET MESSY

Bet you already know that your fingers and hands can be used like paintbrushes. There are few activities more fun than finger painting.

Finger painting probably is the first kind of painting ever to have existed. It's as easy as dipping your hand in some paint and smearing it on a sheet of paper. There's even a special kind of paint that's just for finger painting and is easy to wash off.

Kids who finger paint often draw large objects with their hands and fingers. But some older children and adults can make finger paint pictures that look as if they were painted with a brush.

There are some famous painters that use their hands and fingers to paint, including Jackson Pollock, Robert Motherwell, Mark Rothko, and Willhem de Kooning. They call this type of art action painting! What can you create with just your fingers and your hands?

Handprint Butterfly Art

WHAT YOU NEED:
- WHITE POSTER BOARD • WASHABLE PAINTS
- BOWLS FOR PAINT • PIPE CLEANERS
- MARKERS • GLITTER • GLUE • PAPER TOWELS
- SELF-STICK MAGNET STRIP

SKILLS:
CREATIVE INNOVATION

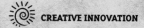

1. Spread out poster board on a flat surface. Put on an old shirt or smock so you don't soil your clothes.

2. Pour paint into bowls large enough to put your hands in.

3. Place your hand in one color of paint and put it on the poster board. Smear it around the paper. Doesn't that feel gooey and good!

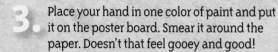

4. Wash and dry your hand and do it again and again with each color. Let the paint dry a little between colors.

5. Sprinkle glitter on the paint and then let the paper dry completely.

6. Cut out the shape of a butterfly from the painted paper. You can make it any size.

7. Glue two pipe cleaners down the middle and bend the ends as antennae.

8. Paint eyes on the butterfly and add a smile using a marker. Attach a self-stick magnet strip to the back and place your beautiful butterfly on a refrigerator or other metal surface.

EVERYDAY ART

The Golden Key

One winter, when a deep snow was lying on the ground a poor Boy had to go out in a sleigh to fetch wood. As soon as he had collected together a sufficient quantity, he thought that before he returned home he would make a fire to warm himself at, because his limbs were so frozen. So sweeping the snow away he made a clear space, and presently found a small gold key. As soon as he picked it up, he began to think that where there was a key there must also be a lock; and digging in the earth he found a small iron chest. "I hope the key will fit," thought he to himself; "there are certainly great treasures in the box!" He looked all over it, but could not find any key-hole; till at last he did discover one, which was, however, so small, that it could scarcely be seen. He tried the key, and behold! It fitted exactly. Then he turned it once round, and now we must wait until he has quite unlocked it, and lifted the lid up, and then we shall learn what wonderful treasures were in the chest!

JACOB AND WILHELM GRIMM

"Consistency is the last refuge of the unimaginative."

OSCAR WILDE

"The world is but a canvas to our imaginations."

HENRY DAVID THOREAU

◄ *DON'T FORGET TO WASH MY BLANKET*
BY DELLA WELLS

EVERYDAY ART
RECYCLED FUN

Toilet paper and paper towel rolls turn into swords. Old pillowcases become capes. Wire twists off big green trash bags make beautiful necklaces. Wooden thread spools become slinky snakes. Paper cups become dancing puppets. Soda cans transform into musical instruments. Everything can be made into something else.

There are artists who make their art out of nothing but found things. Outsider and visionary artists use the simplest things to make all kinds of artwork. Vollis Simpson, a machine repairman, makes beautiful whirligigs from recycled machine parts. Some are over 50 feet (15 m) tall. Artist Della Wells uses fabric, ribbon and buttons to make beautiful pieces of art.

Look around your house. What can you use to make something new? The sky's the limit.

Make a Kooky Creature

WHAT YOU NEED:
- PAPER TOWEL ROLLS • PAINT AND BRUSH
- MASKING TAPE • OLD BATH TOWEL
- GOOGLY EYES • CEREAL BOX
- GLUE OR GLUE GUN • STAPLER • SCISSORS

SKILLS:
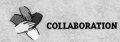
COLLABORATION   CREATIVE INNOVATION

COMMUNICATION

1. Find an empty cereal or popcorn box and a few paper towel/toilet paper rolls. Any size will work. Pull together other recycled things you can find around the house.

2. Lay out your creature parts. The paper rolls make great arms, legs and horns.

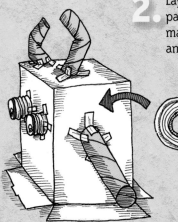

3. Tape the pieces of your creature together with masking tape. Use a lot of tape!

4. Paint your creature any color you imagine.

5. Add extra touches to your monster. For example, what about cotton balls for fur? Glue a googly eye or two on the monster's face. Does your monster have sharp teeth? What could you make these out of?

6. To make hair from an old bath towel, cut long strips of fabric. Staple or glue them to your creature.

Let it dry and go scare your mom!

FROM THE EARTH

Four Breaths

Waikiki coconuts floating on the ocean
Following the currents
Under and over and under...
Great shadow turtles pop up with the surf
Reflecting lunar light and a luxury liner.
At night, jellyfish fill the sky.
Sea foaming clouds
Breathe in and out breaking
Over white and brown-skinned
Surfers paddling like wet dogs.
Shark fins slice like wind down the edge,
Blue water and sunrises, circling the
Chanting, and providing the strength
To return...
Erase your errors in the waters.
Walk back toward the ocean...
Walk back toward the ocean...
Ha, breath; *Ha*, life; *Ha*, beauty
Ha –

JOHN R. HERSHMAN

We are the stars which sing,
We sing with our light;
We are the birds of fire,
We fly over the sky.
We look down on the mountains
This is the song of the stars.

ALGONQUIAN POEM

"We stand
somewhere
between the
mountain
and the ant."
ONONDAGA SAYING

The Arrow and the Song

I shot an arrow in the air;
It fell to earth, I knew not where;
For, so swiftly it flew, the sight
Could not follow it in its flight.

I breathed a song into the air;
It fell to earth, I knew not where;
For who has sight so keen and strong
That it can follow the flight of song?

Long, long afterwards, in an oak
I found the arrow, still unbroken;
And the song, from beginning to end,
I found again in the heart of a friend.

HENRY W. LONGFELLOW

◀ *LITTLE AMERICAN BEAUTY*
BY JEAN HILDEBRANT

FROM THE EARTH
CLAY CREATIONS

Native Americans have a special gift for making things from the earth.

Many years ago some American Indians lived in pueblos, houses built from clay and mud. They made beautiful pots and containers to use everyday. Modern Indians continue the traditions of their ancestors, and create beautiful pottery art.

Some of these Indian potters are known for using a simple process called coiling to form their pottery. Many potters paint their work in gorgeous geometric designs.

These designs are often special to a particular Indian nation, or tribe.

Imagine what it would feel like to make a pot. What would you use it for? What designs would you make to represent you?

Make a Clay Coil Pot

WHAT YOU NEED:
- GRAY OR RED CLAY
- WAX PAPER
- TEMPERA PAINT
- PAINTBRUSH • WATER
- SPONGE (OPTIONAL)

SKILLS:

 CONTENT

 CREATIVE INNOVATION

1. On top of the wax paper, use the heels of your hands to press down on the clay, pushing it away from your body in a rolling motion. This is called kneading. Continue kneading until the clay is soft. Add a little water to the clay if needed.

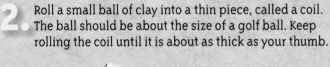

2. Roll a small ball of clay into a thin piece, called a coil. The ball should be about the size of a golf ball. Keep rolling the coil until it is about as thick as your thumb.

3. Roll the coil into a circle on the wax paper to create the base of your pot.

4. Make another coil and wind it around the edges of the base to make sides.

5. Keep adding coils on the sides until it is as tall as you like.

6. Smear the outside of the coils together to create smooth sides on the pot. You can use a damp sponge to help. Let the pot dry in the sun or overnight.

7. Paint designs on your pot and let it dry. Put it on display for your family and friends!

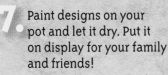

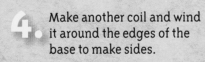

MAGIC AND MAKE-BELIEVE

Imagine a world
filled with
wonder and awe.

ANYTHING'S POSSIBLE

All Day Long

All day long in fog and wind,
The waves have flung their
    beating crests
Against the palisades of adamant.
My boy, he went to sea, long and
    long ago,
Curls of brown were slipping
underneath his cap,
He looked at me from blue and
    steely eyes;
Natty, straight and true, he
    stepped away,
My boy, he went to sea.
All day long in fog and wind,
The waves have flung their
    beating crests
Against the palisades of adamant.

CARL SANDBURG

"If I had a world of my own, everything would be nonsense. Nothing would be what it is, because everything would be what it isn't. And contrary wise, what is, it wouldn't be. And what it wouldn't be, it would. You see?"

LEWIS CARROLL

"Curiosity is, in great and generous minds, the first passion and the last."

SAMUEL JOHNSON

◀ THE LITTLE EXPLORER
BY ELIZABETH SAYLES

ANYTHING'S POSSIBLE
IMAGINE THAT

At night, it's a warm and cozy bed. During the day, at playtime, it becomes a spaceship flying to distant galaxies fast enough to allow you to visit some faraway planet yet return to Earth just in time for dinner.

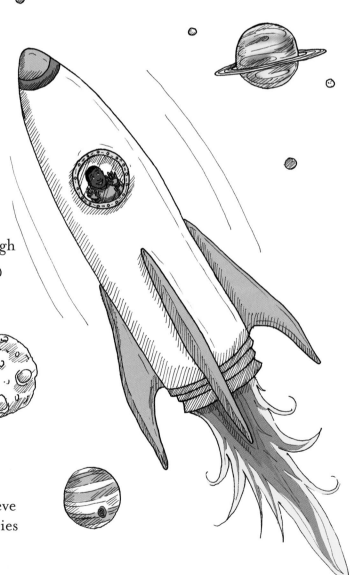

It's fun to turn our everyday world into a land of make-believe. All it takes is a little imagination! Your closet can become a castle that you, the knight, stand by, guarding the king and queen from the evil dragon.

Your basement can be a patchy forest that you, the heroine or hero, must ride through on your trusted stallion to rescue the prince who has fallen under the evil witch's curse.

Your attic can be a lighthouse that you patrol throughout the evening, navigating vessels safely through rugged waters.

Do you have a favorite make-believe story? The best make-believe stories live in your imagination.

Make-Believe Play

WHAT YOU NEED:
- HATS • OLD JEWELRY
- FABRIC • PROPS

SKILLS:

 COLLABORATION   CRITICAL THINKING

COMMUNICATION   CREATIVE INNOVATION

CONTENT CONFIDENCE

1. Imagine you can be anything! A doctor, fireman, ballerina, princess, knight and more!

2. Look around your house for things you can use to create a perfect costume for your character.

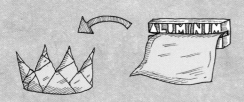

3. Be creative and look for interesting things. It's great fun to put together the perfect outfit. You can make things, too; like a crown out of aluminum foil, a wand from a wooden kitchen spoon, or the hose from a vacuum cleaner.

4. Now think about what you need to make-believe. Maybe a tea set, a stage, or a stuffed animal patient?

5. Pretend and play, letting your imagination take you to another world.

DREAM A LITTLE DREAM

Twinkle, Twinkle, Little Star

Twinkle, twinkle, little star
How I wonder what you are!
Up above the world so high,
Like a diamond in the sky!
When the blazing sun is gone,
When he nothing shines upon,
Then you show your little light,
Twinkle, twinkle, all the night.
Then the traveller in the dark,
Thanks you for your tiny spark,
He could not see which way to go,
If you did not twinkle so.
In the dark blue sky you keep,
And often through my curtains peep,
For you never shut your eye,
Till the sun is in the sky.
As your bright and tiny spark,
Lights the traveller in the dark,
Though I know not what you are,
Twinkle, twinkle, little star

ENGLISH NURSERY RHYME

"Twenty years from now you will be more disappointed by the things that you didn't do than by the ones you did do. So throw off the bowlines. Sail away from the safe harbor. Catch the trade winds in your sails. Explore. Dream. Discover."

MARK TWAIN

"Nothing happens unless first we dream."

CARL SANDBURG

◀ *THE GIANT*
BY NEWELL CONVERS WYETH

DREAM A LITTLE DREAM
WHAT IF...

Daydreaming is when we use our imagination to think of fun things to do and be. The beauty of daydreams is that nothing is impossible. Sometimes we think about good things that have happened to us, or things we want to happen, even things we know can't happen but are fun to think about anyway.

Daydreams are different from dreams we have at night or when we nap. With daydreaming, we can choose where to send our minds.

Some people think daydreaming is bad. They say that people who do so are simply being lazy. But people who study daydreams say they're good for us. They can make us feel better when we are sad. And they can even keep us from being bored.

Some brain scientists call daydreaming "mind-wandering." They are interested in knowing why and how we can lose ourselves in our own thoughts and ideas. Other researchers are studying the power of daydreaming yourself winning a race or doing well at school. It seems that envisioning an outcome helps to make it come true.

Tips for Daydreaming

WHAT YOU NEED:
- YOURSELF • TIME
- A QUIET PLACE

SKILLS:

 CONTENT

 CONFIDENCE

 CREATIVE INNOVATION

1. Find a Quiet Place
Not everyone needs a quiet place to daydream, but it helps.

2. Relax
Daydreaming is a little like meditation. Give yourself some time to unwind. It lets your mind take a break—like a mini-vacation. Take a deep breath and let all of your muscles relax.

3. Watch What Comes to Mind
You never know what might come into your brain when you let your mind wander. Try not to think too hard. Just see what your mind sees. Close your eyes and open your mind.

4. Remember a Memory
Try remembering something that happened to you. How does it make you feel?

5. Make a New Idea
Imagine you can make any wish come true. What would it be?

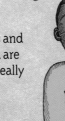

6. If You Could Say Anything
Daydream about your friends and people you love. Imagine you are telling them something you really want them to know.

7. Boost Your Confidence
Daydream doing great at school, winning at a race or anything else. Olympic athletes and performers daydream just like this to help them enhance their performance.

8. When You Are Bored
Daydream when you are bored. Waiting in line, riding in the car or when you are waiting for your parents to take you somewhere and they are moving slowly!

FAIRY MAGIC

Cherry-Time

When I sound the fairy call,
Gather here in silent meeting,
Chin to knee on the orchard
wall,
Cooled with dew and cherries
eating.
Merry, merry, Take a cherry
Mine are sounder,
Mine are rounder
Mine are sweeter,
For the eater
When the dews fall.
And you'll be fairies all.

ROBERT GRAVES

The Fairy Song

Over hill, over dale,
Thorough bush, thorough brier,
Over park, over pale,
Thorough flood, thorough fire!
I do wander everywhere,
Swifter than the moon's sphere;
And I serve the Fairy Queen,
To dew her orbs upon the green;
The cowslips tall her pensioners be;
In their gold coats spots you see;
Those be rubies, fairy favours;
In those freckles live their savours;
I must go seek some dew-drops here,
And hang a pearl in every cowslip's ear.

WILLIAM SHAKESPEARE

"Every time a child says, 'I don't
believe in fairies' there is a fairy
somewhere that falls down dead."

JAMES MATTHEW BARRIE

◀ *MIDSUMMER EVE*
BY EDWARD ROBERT HUGHES

FAIRY MAGIC
OH TO BE A FAIRY!

To fly, to wish, to dance. Have you ever seen a fairy? Maybe when you first wake up. Perhaps out of the corner of your eye. Or have you ever lost something only to find it later? Could a fairy have borrowed it?

Fairies (and elves) seem to show up in lots of tales from around the world. There are many kinds of fairies, too. You probably know about the tooth fairy and Tinker Bell, but there are flower fairies, bedtime fairies, princess fairies and more. Another well-known fairy is the Fairy Godmother in the story, "Cinderella."

Fairies live indoors and outside, making their houses in tree trunks, under big bushes, in attics and closets. Fairies love really soft things like shiny fabric and cotton balls.

No one really knows where fairies come from. Stories about them can be heard in almost every country around the world. We do know that all fairies can make magic and that fairy magic is almost always good. They are happy to grant your wishes, and they love to dance and sing.

Fairy magic is what helps us to see a world where anything is possible. Look around; you never know where you will see a fairy.

Make a Fairy House

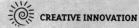

WHAT YOU NEED:
- FABRIC • TWIGS • ACORNS
- STRING • FLOWERS
- CARDBOARD BOX OR MILK CARTON

SKILLS:

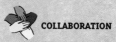 COLLABORATION

CREATIVE INNOVATION

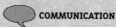 COMMUNICATION

1. Look for a place on a bookshelf, under a bed, beneath a tree, or even behind a bush to find a place to make your fairy house.

2. Find things you can use to build your fairy house plus furniture, and other things they will need to put inside it. Doll furniture, miniature tools, fabric, flowers, acorns, twigs and string are all great. Remember fairy houses come in all shapes and sizes—fat, short, tall, skinny.

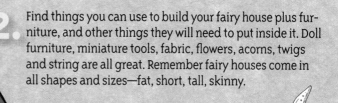

3. Look for something that can become the base of the house. A cardboard box or milk carton could work.

4. Construct the house so it is easy for your fairy friends to go in and out. Try building little furniture using pieces of wood or stones. Small cardboard boxes are great for tables. Use clay to make dishes. What about making the roof out of fabric or adding wallpaper? Maybe you need a rug, too.

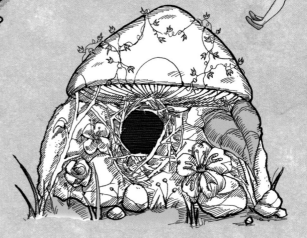

5. Fairies love sweet tea and cookies. Bring some to their house and have some yourself. Remember fairies are neat and rarely disturb their surroundings so it might be difficult to know when they've been in the house. You'll have to use your imagination to see the signs.

MEDIEVAL QUEST

Why Dragons?

The smoke still hangs heavily over
   the meadow,
Circling down from the mouth
   of the cave,
While kneeling in prayer, full armored
   and haloed,
The lone knight is feeling
   uncertainly brave.

The promise of victory sung in
   the churches,
Is hardly a murmur out here in the air.
All that he hears is the thud of this
   faint heart
Echoing growls of the beast in its lair.

The steel of his armor would
   flash in the sunlight,
Except that the smoke has quite hidden
   the sky.
The red of the cross on his breast
   should sustain him,
Except—he suspects—it's a perfect
   bull's-eye.

The folk of the village who bet
   on the outcome
Have somehow all fled from the
   scene in dismay.
They'll likely return in a fortnight
   or longer,
He doubts that they'll be of much
   help on this day.

And then—with a scream—the fell
   beast of the cavern

Flings its foul body full out of the cave.
The knight forgets prayers and
   churches and haloes
And tries to remember just how
   to be brave.
The webs on the wings of the dragon
   are reddened,
With blood or with sunlight, the knight
   is not sure.
The head of the beast is a silver-
   toothed nightmare,
Its tongue drips a poison for which
   there's no cure.

He thrusts his sword and he pokes
   with his gauntlets,
He knees with he poleyn, kicks out
   with his greave.
He'd happily give all the gold in his pocket
If only the dragon would quietly leave.

There's smoke and there's fire, there's
   wind and there's growling.
There's screams from the knights, and
   his sobs and his cries.
And when the smoke clears, there's
   the sound of dry heaving
As one of the two of them messily dies.

Of course it's the knight who has
   won this hard battle,
Who wins in a poem beaten out on a forge
Of human devising and human invention.
BUT: If there's no dragon—then there's
   no Saint George.

JANE YOLEN

◀ *DRAGON AND BOY*
BY KATHI EMBER

MEDIEVAL QUEST
DRAGON TIME

Dragons are giant, flying, fire-breathing reptiles that appear in folk stories and legends from Europe and Asia. In most tales, they are ferocious. They soar through the sky, burning everything in their path and shaking the ground with their roar.

In some tales, dragons are no match for knights in shining armor. A knight was a warrior soldier from the Middle Ages, and many are said to have waged fierce battles with dragons and emerged triumphant. Saint George and Sir Lancelot of legendary times fought and defeated dragons.

It's fun to pretend to be both dragons (without the fire, of course) and knights. You can use costumes or old clothes to go from your everyday surroundings to a world where human and beast wage thrilling battles.

Throughout literature there have been some very famous dragons. Some, like those in Chinese stories, are fierce. Others—like Puff, the Magic Dragon—are friendly.

Go on a Dragon Hunt

WHAT YOU NEED:
- PAPER, CRAYONS, MARKERS
- MAKE-BELIEVE SWORD
- PILLOWCASE

SKILLS:
 COLLABORATION

 CONTENT

COMMUNICATION

CREATIVE INNOVATION

Note to Parents: Your dragon hunter needs your help for this activity. Create a Dragon Hunting Map for your child. Hide special treats at each location. Be creative. At the end of the hunt, leave a special letter from the dragon and maybe some cookies!

1. Dragon Wanted
Draw a picture of the dragon you are searching for. Does it have a long tail with spikes? Is it green and blue? Does it blow fire or orange juice from its mouth?

2. Dragon Hunting Gear
What do you need to begin your dragon search? Maybe a sword and cape? Find the gear you need and get ready. Put the picture of your dragon in your pocket.

3. Let the Games Begin
Ask your parents for their Dragon Hunting Map. Your adventure awaits. Follow the map clues to see what you can find.

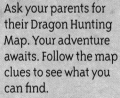

4. Find the Dragon
Did you find the Dragon's letter? Share it with your family and friends.

BE A SUPERHERO

If

If you can keep your head
    when all about you
Are losing theirs and
    blaming it on you;
If you can trust yourself
    when all men doubt you,
But make allowance for
    their doubting too;
If you can wait and not
    be tired by waiting,
Or, being lied about,
    don't deal in lies,
Or, being hated, don't
    give way to hating,
And yet don't look too good,
    nor talk too wise;

If you can dream—and not
    make dreams your master;
If you can think—and not
    make thoughts your aim;
If you can meet with
    triumph and disaster
And treat those two
    imposters just the same;
If you can bear to hear
    the truth you've spoken
Twisted by knaves to make
    a trap for fools,
Or watch the things you gave
    your life to broken,
And stoop and build 'em up
    with wornout tools;

If you can make one heap
    of all your winnings
And risk it on one turn
    of pitch-and-toss,
And lose, and start again
    at your beginnings
And never breath a word
    about your loss;
If you can force your heart
    and nerve and sinew
To serve your turn long
    after they are gone,
And so hold on when
    there is nothing in you
Except the Will which says
    to them: "Hold on";

If you can talk with crowds
    and keep your virtue,
Or walk with kings—nor lose
    the common touch;
If neither foes nor loving
    friends can hurt you;
If all men count with you,
    but none too much;
If you can fill the unforgiving minute
With sixty seconds' worth of
    distance run—
Yours is the Earth and everything
    that's in it,
And—which is more—you'll be
    a Man my son!

RUDYARD KIPLING

◀ *SUPERBOY HERO*
BY MARK MURPHY

BE A SUPERHERO
MY SUPERPOWER
IS...

When you think of a superhero, you might think of someone who can fly through the air like a jet or run faster than a rocket or lift a train off the tracks, even put out a fire with ice-cold breath.

A superhero is a character in a story who uses amazing powers to do good deeds. Superheroes are stronger, faster, or smarter than most humans, which means that one can often do the job of an entire army.

Most people who know about superheroes have a favorite one. Some of the most popular are Superman, Wonder Woman, Spider-Man, and Batman. They appear in comic books, in comic strips, in television shows, and even in movies.

With a little imagination, you can pretend to be a favorite superhero or create your own. Want to give it a try?

How to Be a Superhero

WHAT YOU NEED:
- SUPERHERO ACCESSORIES
- PILLOWCASE • FELT

SKILLS:

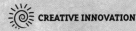 COLLABORATION

CREATIVE INNOVATION

COMMUNICATION

CONFIDENCE

CRITICAL THINKING

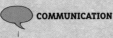
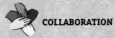

1. Extraordinary Powers
The one thing all superheroes have is an ability that no one else has. It could be something like Spider-Man's webbing or Wolverine's claws. Think about what your superpower might be and choose one.

2. What's in a Name?
Once you know your superpower, you need a name. What will you call yourself?

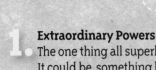

3. Secret Identity
Superheroes don't just walk around every day as superheroes. They have secret identities. What is your secret identity?

4. A Special Costume
All superheroes have a costume they wear so their secret identities are not revealed. For example, many heroes wear masks, capes or caps to cover their heads. Some have special letters on their clothes. What does your costume look like?

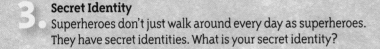
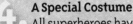

5. Villains and Evil Doers
All superheroes have someone they need to stop from doing harm in the world. Who are your archenemies? What are their powers? What do you need to protect?

6. Base of Operations
Superheroes need a secret place to hide their stuff and a headquarters where they can meet with other superheroes. Batman has a cave. Superman has the Fortress of Solitude. Where are your headquarters?

7. Ready for Action
You never know when danger will strike. Get your superhero stuff ready. Keep it under your bed or in a special drawer. When it is time, you will be ready for action. Practice being a superhero around your house any time you feel like it.

CLANG, CLANG, BANG, BANG

The Ants Go Marching

The ants go marching six by six. Hurrah, hurrah! (Repeat)
The ants go marching six by six, the little one stops to pick up sticks,
And they all go marching down to the ground to get out of the rain.
The ants go marching seven by seven. Hurrah, hurrah! (Repeat)
The ants go marching seven by seven, the little one stops to go to heaven,
And they all go marching down to the ground to get out of the rain.
The ants go marching eight by eight. Hurrah, hurrah! (Repeat)
The ants go marching eight by eight, the little one stops to shut the gate,
And they all go marching down to the ground to get out of the rain.
The ants go marching nine by nine. Hurrah, hurrah! (Repeat)
The ants go marching nine by nine, the little one stops to check the time,
And they all go marching down to the ground to get out of the rain.
The ants go marching ten by ten. Hurrah, hurrah! (Repeat)
The ants go marching ten by ten, the little one stops to say "THE END"
And they all go marching down to the ground to get out of the rain.

CAMP SONG

John Jacob Jingleheimer Schmidt

John Jacob Jingleheimer Schmidt
His name is my name too.
Whenever we go out,
The people always shout,
There goes John Jacob Jingleheimer Schmidt.
Dah dah dah dah, dah dah dah
(Repeat in an infinite loop)

GERMAN CHILDREN'S SONG

◀ *NEW ORLEANS JAZZ MUSICIANS*
BY WOODIE LONG

CLANG, CLANG, BANG, BANG
POTS & PAN BAND

Grab a pot from your kitchen cupboard. Turn it upside down. Take a big ladle and beat it against the pot. Clang! Clang! Clang! Those are some awesome sounds. Some grown-ups might call it noise, but make a steady beat out of it, and you've got music.

Don't believe it? Well, there's a theater group called Stomp! They put on an amazing music show with pots, pans, skillets, ladles, wooden and metal spoons, and tea kettles. They do it so well that they make it sound like real music instruments. Some other famous musicians play with washboards, spoons, and dishpans.

Maybe you and your friends can get together and form a band. Start out with simple, light taps that everyone can do to get the beat, then make it faster and louder, with different beats mixed in. Soon you'll have the best band a kitchen has ever made!

So keep clanging! First, however, ask a grown-up's permission, and she or he will probably give you an old pot that is not being used much anymore. You can use anything for drumsticks: plastic spoons, markers, pencils, chopsticks, whatever you can hold in two hands.

Create Your Own Music

WHAT YOU NEED:
- POTS AND PANS
- WOODEN SPOONS
- EMPTY SODA CANS
- PENNIES
- DUCT TAPE
- CD OR OTHER MUSIC PLAYER

SKILLS:
COLLABORATION

CREATIVE INNOVATION

COMMUNICATION

CONFIDENCE

CONTENT

1. Find kitchen supplies to make percussion instruments and sounds. Here are some ideas. Experiment with different forks, spoons, pot and lid sizes to get different sounds.

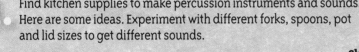

Chimes: Forks

Shaker: Soda can with pennies inside (tape over opening with duct tape)

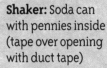

Cymbals: Two metal lids

Drums: Metal pots and wooden spoons

Gongs: Cookie sheet and mallet

2. Gather a group of friends and family. Make some noise!

3. Turn on a CD or iPod music with a strong percussion beat as loud as you can and play along.

4. Take your pots and pan band on the road! Start a parade!

magic and make-believe 87

LET'S PUT ON A SHOW

Ladies and Jellyspoons

I come before you
to stand behind you
And tell you something
I know nothing about.

Next Thursday,
which is Good Friday,
there will be a Mothers meeting,
for Fathers only.

Wear your best clothes
if you haven't any,
and if you can come,
please stay at home.

Admission's free
pay at the door.
Take a seat
and sit on the floor.
It makes no difference
where you sit
The man in the gallery's
sure to spit.

AUTHOR UNKNOWN

"The thing about performance, even if it's only an illusion, is that it is a celebration of the fact that we do contain within ourselves infinite possibilities."

SYDNEY SMITH

"All the world's a stage, And all the men and women merely players."

WILLIAM SHAKESPEARE

LET'S PUT ON A SHOW
INTRODUCING...

It's exciting to watch a movie, a television show, or a play. But it's even more fun putting on your own show.

Putting on a show is a good way for you and your friends to use your imagination and talent.

The first thing you'll need to do is decide what kind of show you want to make. Will it be a fairy tale? Or maybe a story about dungeons and dragons? Will you do a story from a book that your parents read to you at bedtime? Or will you act out your favorite TV show or movie? What about a musical or a dance number? You could even sing a favorite song.

Once you decide the kind of show you would like to do, you will need actors to play the part of each character in the show. Everyone can be a character; some characters have words to say (called lines), while other characters can make noises, like the roar of a lion.

Showtime Ideas

WHAT YOU NEED:
- DRESS-UP COSTUMES
- MAKE-BELIEVE STAGE
- FRIENDS AND FAMILY
- iPOD OR CDS
- PAPER AND MARKERS

SKILLS:

COLLABORATION

CRITICAL THINKING

COMMUNICATION

CREATIVE INNOVATION

CONTENT

CONFIDENCE

1. Envision the Show
Do you want to sing, dance, read a poem, tell a story, do a magic trick or act out a play? It's up to you. It's your show!

2. Make a Stage
Find a place in your house or even outside to perform your show. Set up chairs for your audience. Think about what you need on your stage. Make sure you have access to a CD player if you need recorded music.

Stage

3. Practice, Practice, Practice
Once you know what's in the show, practice. This will help you feel more confident when you have an audience in front of you.

Audience

4. Create a Costume
What will you wear? Do you need makeup? Do you need special shoes or clothes?

5. Invite an Audience
Make tickets for your show and give them to friends and family. Add the time and location on the ticket.

6. Make a Program
Create a program for your audience. List performers and what they will be performing.

7. Dressing Room
Take some time to get ready. Create a dressing room where you can prepare!

8. It's Showtime
Your audience has arrived and it's time to go! Remember to take a bow at the end of your performance.

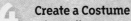
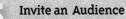

SILLY TIME

All Around the Mulberry Bush

All around the mulberry bush
The Monkey chased the weasel.
The monkey thought 'twas all in fun.
Pop! goes the weasel.

A penny for a spool of thread,
A penny for a needle.
That's the way the money goes.
Pop! Goes the weasel.

Up and down the City Road,
In and out of the Eagle,
That's the way the money goes.
Pop! Goes the weasel.

Half a pound of tuppernney rice,
Half a pound of treacle,
Mix up and make it nice,
Pop! Goes the weasel.

NURSERY RHYME

Ring Around the Roses

Ring around the roses
A pocket full of posies
Ashes, ashes
We all fall down.

MOTHER GOOSE
NURSERY RHYME

Hickory Dickory Dock

Hickory, dickory, dock,
the mouse ran up the clock.
The clock struck one,
the mouse ran down,
hickory, dickory, dock.

ENGLISH NURSERY RHYME

"Against the assault
of laughter nothing
can stand."

MARK TWAIN

◄ *CHILDREN DANCING WITH ANIMALS*
BY VALERIE CIS

SILLY TIME
GIGGLE, GIGGLE

There are so many wonderfully silly things to do, and there's no right way or wrong way to create silly time. You can be silly anytime, too, like when you are waking up from a nap, feeling grumpy, or just need a break from what you are doing.

Laughing is one of the best ways to make yourself feel good from the inside out! Smiling is also a sure-fire way to get the giggling going. In fact a smile is a great way to make new friends, too. Try smiling and see what happens.

Silly-time activities can be played anywhere—in the car, around the dinner table, or on a rainy afternoon.

Psychologists actually study laughter and have learned some pretty funny things. For example, people laughed more 40 years ago, and laughter improves relationships and friendships, making us feel closer. Laughter also has positive effects on our health—physical and mental.

Time to get serious about being silly!

Silly Things to Do

WHAT YOU NEED:
- FRIENDS AND FAMILY

SKILLS:
 COLLABORATION
CONTENT
COMMUNICATION
CREATIVE INNOVATION

1. No Laughing Competition
Whatever you do—don't laugh! That is the only rule of this silly thing to do. But you have to do everything you can think of to make others laugh. The winner is the person who does not laugh!

2. Laugh Out Loud Contest
Try creating a new laugh. Can you laugh like an evil villain? Can you laugh like a monkey? How long is your loudest laugh?

3. Use Your Mouth
Can you touch your tongue to the tip of your nose? Can you whistle a song through your tongue? Can you whistle at all? Find people that can and get them to teach you!

4. Animal Imitation
Pretend you are an animal. What about an elephant? Create a pretend trunk; walk and roar like an elephant. Be a monkey. How do monkeys walk? What about a snake? Could you be a slinky snake, hissing your way across the floor?

5. Snap Your Fingers
Do you know how? Hold your middle finger up against your thumb and quickly snap it. You should hear a cool clicking sound. Practice until you get really great at it.

6. Make a Face
Do you have a really funny face? Make one up. Squint your eyes, stick out your tongue, cross your eyes, raise an eyebrow. Pucker your lips and stick out your tongue. Take a picture of your silly face!

"silly face"

YUMMY
IN MY TUMMY

Food for thought, food for friends, food for fun!

COMFORT FOOD

Stone Soup

A very long time ago there was a great famine. People were scared and jealously protected whatever food they could find. One day a wandering soldier came into the village and explained that he planned to stay for the night.

"There's no food in the whole town," he was told. "Better keep moving on."

"No worries, I have everything I need," he said. "In fact, I am going to make some stone soup to share with all of you." With that, he pulled out a large pot, filled it with water, and built a fire under it. Then, carefully, he took a simple round stone from a velvet pouch and dropped it in the water.

By now, most of the villagers had come to see for themselves the rumor of soup cooking in the square. The soldier smelled the "broth" as he carefully stirred the pot. Slowly? Soon the villagers could smell soup, too.

One by one, villagers approached the soldier, each with a small piece of food to put in the soup. First came cabbage and then rice. Each time a new nibble of food was added the soldier laughed, "This will be the best soup yet."

Things continued just this way — The village butcher found some beef and others brought potatoes, onions, carrots and mushrooms until there was a delicious meal for all.

The villagers were delighted and very satisfied by the wonderful soup and were amazed that it was made from a stone. They offered the soldier money to buy this special rock but the soldier refused, leaving early the next morning to continue his journey.

The villagers never understood how that soup really came to be so good, but you know, don't you?

FAIRY TALE

The Mock Turtle's Song

Beautiful soup, so rich and green,
Waiting in a hot tureen!
Who for such dainties would
    not stoop?
Soup of the evening, beautiful Soup!
Soup of the evening, beautiful Soup!
Beau--ootiful Soo--oop!
Beau--ootiful Soo--oop!
Soo--oop of the e--e--evening,
Beautiful, beautiful Soup.

LEWIS CARROLL

◀ *THANKSGIVING DINNER*
BY BERNICE SIMS

COMFORT FOOD
SOUP & STEW

There is nothing more soothing than soup. Chicken noodle. Spicy tomato. Split pea. Minestrone. New England clam chowder. Beef stew. These are some of the best-tasting soups, and on a cold autumn or winter day, they are just what you need to feel warm inside. Did you know Americans sip over 10 billion bowls of soup every year?

Most soup is a food made of water, with all sorts of ingredients mixed in, such as vegetables, meat, noodles, and spices.

In some cultures soup is served as breakfast. In Japan miso soup or fish broth with rice is popular.

Years ago, sipping soup was something that many families did during the holidays. Some newspapers even printed ingredients for the best sipping soups.

Try starting a "big bowl night" where everyone creates their favorite soup. Soups are the perfect invention. Anything can go into a soup, and the results are almost always wonderful.

Simple Soup Recipes

BROCCOLI TREE CHEESE SOUP

INGREDIENTS:
2 cups (473 ml) water
3 cups (450 g) broccoli
1/4 cup (40 g) chopped
   onion
1 teaspoon (5 ml) salt
Pinch of curry powder
1 cup (237 ml) milk
1 cup (237 ml) water
1 1/2 tablespoons (22.5 ml) cornstarch
1/2 cup (120 g) American cheese—cut into
small pieces

SKILLS:

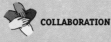 COLLABORATION   CONTENT

COMMUNICATION   CREATIVE INNOVATION

1. Bring 2 cups (473 ml) water to a boil.
   Add broccoli, onions, salt, and curry powder.
   Cook, covered, until almost tender.
2. Mix milk, water, and cornstarch together.
   Add to partially cooked vegetables.
3. Cook over medium heat, stirring often,
   until thickened.
4. Add cheese and stir until melted. Add more
   water if too thick.

SALSA SOUP

INGREDIENTS:
1 pound (454 g) extra lean ground beef
4 cups (946 ml) water
5 potatoes, peeled and chopped
1 medium onion, chopped
2 small carrots, chopped
1 envelope dry onion soup mix
1 16-oz (473-ml) jar chunky salsa

1. Brown the meat in a skillet over medium heat
   and drain.
2. Pour the water into large pot and add the
   ground beef, potatoes, onion, and carrots.
3. Sprinkle the dry onion soup mix over
   the vegetables and meat.
4. Mix in the salsa thoroughly.
5. Cover and cook on low for about 30 minutes.

SILLY CHICKEN RICE SOUP

INGREDIENTS:
6 cups (1.4 l) of chicken broth
1 cup (150 g) cooked chicken
1 cup (190 g) uncooked rice
1 3/4 cup (310 g) fresh chopped vegetables
1/2 teaspoon (2.5 ml) garlic powder
1/4 teaspoon (1.25 ml) each of pepper and salt

1. Place the cooked chicken in a large saucepan.
2. Add the broth and uncooked rice. Cover the pan.
3. Bring the broth and rice to a boil.
4. Cover the pan, and turn the heat to low.
5. Stir occasionally while simmering for 15 minutes.
6. Add the chopped vegetables and seasonings.
7. Simmer for another 10 to 15 minutes until the
   vegetables are tender.

Make sure grown-ups help with the cooking!

KITCHEN CHEMISTRY

Little Miss Muffet

Little Miss Muffet
Sat on a tuffet,
Eating some curds and whey.
Along came a spider,
And sat down beside her,
And frightened Miss Muffet away.

NURSERY RHYME

Little Tom Tucker

Little Tom Tucker Sings for his supper.
What shall he eat?
White bread and butter.
How will he cut it
Without e'er a knife?
How will he be married?
Without e'er a wife?

NURSERY RHYME

Oats, Peas, Beans, and Barley Grow

Oats, peas, beans, and barley grow,
Oats, peas, beans, and barley grow,
Can you or I or anyone know
How oats, peas, beans, and barley grow?

First the farmer sows his seed,
Stands erect and takes his ease,
He stamps his foot and claps his hands,
And turns around to view his lands.

Next the farmer waters the seed,
Stands erect and takes his ease,
He stamps his foot and claps his hands,
And turns around to view his lands.

Next the farmer hoes the weeds,
Stands erect and takes his ease,
He stamps his foot and claps his hands,
And turns around to view his lands.

Last the farmer harvests his seed,
Stands erect and takes his ease,
He stamps his foot and claps his hands,
And turns around to view his lands.

FOLK SONG

◀ *THE BIRTHDAY*
BY KONSTANTIN FEDOROVICH BOGAEVSKY

KITCHEN CHEMISTRY
SILLY SANDWICHES

It is believed the modern sandwich was named after John Montagu, 4th Earl of Sandwich. One day he got hungry while playing cards, so he asked for a piece of meat between two slices of bread so he could eat and play at the same time. Others began to order "the same as Sandwich."

Have you ever invented anything? Well, why not try it? Why not invent a peanut butter and caramel popcorn sandwich? For even more taste, sprinkle some cinnamon on top. You've had a chicken salad sandwich and a tuna salad sandwich, why not fruit salad sandwich?

Silly sandwiches are a fun way to enjoy different flavors of foods. You can combine sweet with salty, sour with tangy or gooey with creamy.

The most popular sandwich in the U.S. is reported to be a simple ham sandwich. The second is bacon, lettuce, and tomato. It is estimated that Americans eat 300 million sandwiches a day.

The largest sandwich ever made weighed 5,440 pounds (2,468 kg). It was made in 2005 at Wild Woody's Chill and Grill in Roseville, Michigan.

So, what would you like in your sandwich today? If you could have your most favorite things in a sandwich what would they be?

Invent a Sandwich

WHAT YOU NEED:
- WHATEVER IS IN YOUR REFRIGERATOR AND CABINETS

SKILLS:

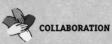

COLLABORATION

CONTENT

COMMUNICATION

CREATIVE INNOVATION

Be sure to ask a grown-up for help to create a sandwich.

Outside Ideas
By definition a sandwich is something between two somethings. So here are some suggestions for the outside:
- Wheat, white, rye, or pumpernickel bread
- Hot dog bun, hamburger bun, dinner roll
- Taco shell
- Tortilla

Inside Ideas
Mix and match anything you love. Try putting things together you have never tasted before.
- Lunch meat
- Fruit
- Cheese
- Peanut butter
- Tuna, chicken, turkey
- Bacon
- Eggs
- Tofu
- Mashed potatoes
- Dressing
- Nuts

Extras
For a little extra spice why not try:
- Mayonnaise
- Mustard
- Lemon juice
- Spices like chives, thyme, sage, garlic
- Maple syrup
- Honey
- Oil
- Butter
- Veggies
- Different kinds of lettuce
- Soy sauce
- Tomato sauce
- Applesauce
- Pickles
- Seeds and sprouts
- Barbecue sauce

Techniques and Preparations
Here are some other things to consider:
- Toast it
- Bake it
- Dip it in egg and sauté in butter
- Grill with butter
- Eat it cold
- Microwave it

Now that you have invented a new sandwich, you need to name it!

HOT & COLD

Simple Simon Met a Pieman

Simple Simon met a pieman,
Going to the fair;
Says Simple Simon to the pieman,
Let me taste your ware.
Says the pieman to Simple Simon,
Show me first your penny;
Says Simple Simon to the pieman,
Indeed I have not any.
Simple Simon went a-fishing,
For to catch a whale;
All the water he had got,
Was in his mother's pail.
Simple Simon went to look
If plums grew on a thistle;
He pricked his fingers very much,
Which made poor Simon whistle.

MOTHER GOOSE
NURSERY RHYME

Animal Crackers

Animal crackers and cocoa to drink,
That is the finest of suppers I think;
When I'm grown up and can have
    what I please
I think I shall always insist upon these.
What do YOU choose when you're
    offered a treat?
When Mother says, "What would you
    like best to eat?"
Is it waffles and syrup, or
    cinnamon toast?
It's cocoa and animals that I love most!
The kitchen's the cosiest place
    that I know;
The kettle is singing, the stove is aglow,
And there in the twilight,
    how jolly to see
The cocoa and animals waiting for me.
Daddy and Mother dine later in state,
With Mary to cook for them,
Susan to wait;
But they don't have nearly as
    much fun as I
Who eat in the kitchen with
Nurse standing by;
And Daddy once said, he would
    like to be me
Having cocoa and animals
    once more for tea!

CHRISTOPHER MORLEY

◄ *BAKING*
BY VALERIA DOCAMPO

HOT AND COLD
SLURPS & STRAWS

There are many wonderful drinks to drink. And they can be made to be hot or cold, sweet or sour, chunky or smooth. So you can sip and slurp your drink.

Drinks can be made from almost anything! Lemons make lemonade. Ice tea may be made from tea bags filled with dried leaves. Did you know soda is made from sparkling water, corn syrup, and flavoring? Root beer was originally made using the sassafras plant.

Inventing drinks is a lot of fun. Ginger ale was invented in Ireland in the 1850s. Dr. John S. Pemberton invented Coca-Cola in Atlanta, Georgia, in 1886 from a medicinal drink he prescribed. And Pepsi-Cola followed in 1898. The rest is history.

Did you know that drinking straws have been used for hundreds of years? Some of the first straws were not made but came from long rye grass. In 1888, inventor Marvin Stone began selling straws that he created by wrapping paper around a pencil and then gluing the paper together.

Drink Concoctions

Here are some great drinks for any occasion. Why not use these for inspiration and create your own special drink! Don't forget to ask a grown-up for help in the kitchen.

SKILLS:

 COLLABORATION

 CONTENT

COMMUNICATION

CREATIVE INNOVATION

HOT DRINKS

INSTANT HOT CHOCOLATE

INGREDIENTS
1 chocolate bar
1 cup (237 ml) of milk
Whipped cream
Nutmeg

1. Break chocolate bar into little bits and melt in sauce pan.
2. Add milk and stir.
3. Pour in cup and put a heaping spoon of whipped cream on top.
4. Sprinkle with nutmeg.

HOT CIDER

INGREDIENTS
Apple cider
Cinnamon stick
Dash of vanilla

1. Heat apple cider in a pot with cinnamon stick.
2. Pour in cup when heated. Add a dash of vanilla and sip on a cold day!

COLD DRINKS

KIWI MELON DRINK
(NEED BLENDER)

INGREDIENTS
2 kiwifruit, peeled
1 cup (237 ml) honeydew melon cubes
2 tablespoons sugar

Blend together for one minute.

CHERRY LIMEADE

INGREDIENTS
1/2 cup (118 ml) lemon lime soda
2 limes
1 teaspoon cherry juice
1 maraschino cherry

1. Rinse limes, cut in half, and squeeze juice into a tall glass.
2. Add soda and cherry juice and stir well.
3. Add a maraschino cherry on top for fun.

FROZEN DRINKS

FRUITY SMOOTHIE
(NEED BLENDER)

INGREDIENTS
1 cup (237 ml) nonfat vanilla or plain yogurt or lowfat milk
1/4 teaspoon (1.25 ml) vanilla
2 ice cubes
Any fruit that you want to use (fresh or frozen)

1. Rinse fruit and take off any stems.
2. Cut up fruits such as strawberries, bananas, and mangos.
3. Add the rest of the ingredients.
4. Blend for about 30 to 40 seconds or until smooth and creamy.
5. Pour into glasses and enjoy!

SWEETS FOR THE SWEET

Pat-a-Cake

Pat-a-cake, pat-a-cake, baker's man.
Bake me a cake as fast as you can;
Pat it and prick it and mark it with B,
Put it in the oven for baby and me.

Patty cake, patty cake, baker's man.
Bake me a cake as fast as you can;
Roll it up, roll it up;
And throw it in a pan!
Patty cake, patty cake, baker's man.

ENGLISH NURSERY RHYME

Blueberries

Blueberries as big as the end
    of your thumb,
Real sky-blue, and heavy, and
    ready to drum
In the cavernous pail of the
    first one to come!
And all ripe together, not
    some of them green
And some of them ripe! You ought to
    have seen!

ROBERT FROST

Animal Crackers in My Tea

Animal crackers in my tea
Mother says are good for me
Father says will never do
To have a zoo inside of you

AUTHOR UNKNOWN

Oranges and Lemons

Oranges and lemons
Say the bells of St. Clement's.
You owe me five farthings
Say the bells of St. Martin's.
When will you pay me?
Say the bells of Old Bailey.
When I grow rich,
Say the bells of Shoreditch.
When will that be?
Says the bells of Stepney.
I do not know,
Says the great bell of Bow.

ENGLISH NURSERY RHYME

◀ *SUNDAY MORNING*
BY HYACINTH MANNING

SWEETS FOR THE SWEET
SO GOOD

We all have our favorite sweets. Hard candy, chewy candy, chocolate-chip cookies, fruit pies, bubble gum, cupcakes, ice cream and milkshakes, to name a few. Fruits are also great treats. What about strawberries, raspberries, bananas, raisins, and oranges? They taste so sweet.

There are some sweets that you see mostly on holidays, like chocolate Easter bunnies or peppermint candy canes for hanging on Christmas trees. Some parents give their children candy for being good. And what would Halloween be without a bag full of trick-or-treat goodies?

What's your favorite treat?

Recipes for Perfect Treats

BANANA PUDDING

INGREDIENTS
1 package vanilla pudding
1 cup (237 ml) milk
2 cups (473 ml) whipped cream
36 vanilla wafers
2 sliced bananas

1. Add milk to pudding and mix.
2. Fold in whipped cream.
3. Layer, starting with wafers on the bottom, then bananas and pudding mixture, in a bowl.
4. Top with whipped cream.
5. Chill before serving.

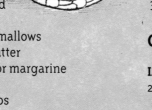

GRANOLA BARS

INGREDIENTS
2 cups (180 g) old fashioned oats
3 cups (400 g) mini marshmallows
1/2 cup (118.5 ml) peanut butter
3 teaspoons (15 ml) butter or margarine
1 cup (150 g) raisins
1/2 cup (75 g) chocolate chips

1. Spread oats out on an ungreased cookie sheet and bake at 350 degrees for 15 minutes; toss often.
2. Cool. Place remaining ingredients, except chocolate chips and raisins, in a saucepan.
3. Cook over low heat, stirring constantly until melted.
4. Remove from heat.
5. Quickly stir in oats and raisins.
6. Remove from stove and stir in chocolate chips.
7. Spread into baking pan.
8. Chill until set. Cut into bars.

SKILLS:

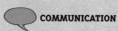 COLLABORATION

 CONTENT

COMMUNICATION

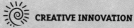 CREATIVE INNOVATION

BAKED APPLES

INGREDIENTS
1 apple, peeled and cored
Cinnamon and sugar to taste
1 tablespoon (15 ml) butter

1. Wrap all of the above tightly in foil and bake at 350 degrees for 10 minutes.
2. Let sit for 3 to 5 minutes until apple is softened.
3. Remove the foil—enjoy!

CHOCOLATE CRACKLES

INGREDIENTS
2 cups (473 ml) chocolate chips, melted over hot water
1 teaspoon (5 ml) butter
About 1 cup (90 g) Rice Crispies
2 tablespoons (30 ml) chopped raisins

1. Combine melted chocolate and butter in a basin.
2. Quickly stir in Rice Crispies and raisins until coated with chocolate.
3. Spoon mixture onto a cookie sheet, 1/2 inch (1.3 cm) thick.
4. Put in fridge or a cool place until set.

Be sure to have a grown-up help you in the kitchen, especially with hot water, stoves, and ovens.

BATHTIME BEDTIME DREAMTIME

The night is filled
with magic...

RUB, A DUB, DUB

My Tub

Water's coming out my spigot
Sittin' here in my tub
Wonder what will come out with it
Something's floating here in my suds.

Chorus
My tub's at the end of a big blue ocean
Attached by pipes you can't see
Fish swimming down in the big blue ocean
Love to come and visit....visit with me.

Gazing at the water tunnel
Hoping to fulfill my wish.
Thinking of my favorite snack time
Peanut butter with my jellyfish.

Look out, here comes my fastball
Heading, right for catcher Sam
Maybe we can make the majors
Working out with Sam the Clam.

Chorus
Sailing, across the water
Charting a really tough course
First prize as I cross the finish
Riding on a green sea horse.

The drainpipe now creates a whirlpool.
The water goes swirling out
Flowing to that magic kingdom
That comes alive through my bathtub spout.

**KATHY HIRSH-PASEK AND
MONA GOLDMAN ZAKHEM**

Rub, a Dub, Dub

Rub-a-dub-dub,
Three men in a tub,
And how do you think
    they got there?
The butcher, the baker,
The candlestick-maker,
They all jumped out of
    a rotten potato,
'Twas enough to make
a man stare.

ENGLISH NURSERY RHYME

"Take a music
bath once or twice
a week for a few
seasons, and you
will find that it is
to the soul what
the water bath is
to the body."

**OLIVER WENDELL
HOLMES, JR.**

◄ *BATHTUB*
BY KATHI EMBER

RUB, A DUB, DUB
BUBBLES, BOATS
AND BATHTUBS

How great to get into the tub after a full day of play and mud! There are bubbles, toy boats that float, plastic tub books and rubber ducks. What's missing? Just add hot water and soap.

Bathtime gives us a chance to create our own little world inside a tub. Pour hot water over bubble bath and you've got mounds of white foam, like tiny islands in the sea for your toy boats to sail through.

Or bubbles could be tall weeds in a marsh that your rubber ducks swim around.

When you're having bathtime, always remember to take as many toys with you as possible. Waterproof toys, of course!

Bathtime is so relaxing and fun. At the end of the day, how great to play one more time in the tub! Check out the activity on the next page for some fun things to do in this watery playground.

Bath Voyages

WHAT YOU NEED:
- BATHTUB • TOWEL • BATH PAINT
- SPONGES • FOAM SHEETS
- PLASTIC COLANDER • GOGGLES
- BUBBLE BATH

SKILLS:

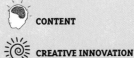

COLLABORATION

CONTENT

COMMUNICATION

CREATIVE INNOVATION

1. Bath Art
You can purchase pre-made bath paints or make your own. Just add one or two drops of food coloring to liquid soap. Parents should help make this concoction.

You can paint yourself or the bathtub wall using sponges or your fingers.

When you are done with your masterpiece, rinse it off right away!

Caution: Food coloring can stain!

2. Bubble Baths, Beards, and Sea Monsters
Add bubble bath mix to your bath and watch the bubbles grow and grow.

Try making a funny hat and beard with the bubbles. What about a five-headed sea monster? Just add bubbles on your toes? And then your nose—just clowning around.

3. Simon Says in the Tub
The tub is a great place to play games, especially if you're taking a bath with a brother or sister. Try Simon Says. Simon Says wash your hair. Simon Says scrub your knees.

4. Tub Fishing
Cut out 12 fish from foam sheets and put them in the tub. See if you can count all 12 as you put them in the plastic colander. How many are green? How many are yellow? How many are sharks?

5. Shampoo Starter
Everyone hates getting soap in their eyes. Why not put on some goggles when you shampoo? You will be amazed how painless it is to wash your hair. Then put your goggled eyes under water and see what lurks beneath the surface—Yikes ... your toes!

bathtime, bedtime, dreamtime

ONCE UPON A TIME
The Fox and the Horse

A farmer had a horse that had been an excellent, faithful servant to him: but he was now grown too old to work; so the farmer would give him nothing more to eat, and said, "I want you no longer, so take yourself off out of my stable; I shall not take you back again until you are stronger than a lion." Then he opened the door and turned him adrift.

The poor horse was very melancholy, and wandered up and down in the wood, seeking some little shelter from the cold wind and rain. Presently a fox met him: "What's the matter, my friend?" said he, "why do you hang down your head and look so lonely and woe-begone?" "Ah!" replied the horse, "justice and avarice never dwell in one house; my master has forgotten all that I have done for him so many years, and because I can no longer work he has turned me adrift, and says unless I become stronger than a lion he will not take me back again; what chance can I have of that? He knows I have none, or he would not talk so."

However, the fox bid him be of good cheer, and said, "I will help you; lie down there, stretch yourself out quite stiff, and pretend to be dead." The horse did as he was told, and the fox went straight to the lion who lived in a cave close by, and said to him, "A little way off lies a dead horse; come with me and you may make an excellent meal of his carcass." The lion was greatly pleased, and set off immediately; and when they came to the horse, the fox said, "You will not be able to eat him comfortably here; I'll tell you what–I will tie you fast to his tail, and then you can draw him to your den, and eat him at your leisure."

This advice pleased the lion, so he laid himself down quietly for the fox to make him fast to the horse. But the fox managed to tie his legs together and bound all so hard and fast that with all his strength he could not set himself free. When the work was done, the fox clapped the horse on the shoulder, and said, "Jip! Dobbin! Jip!" Then up he sprang, and moved off, dragging the lion behind him. The beast began to roar and bellow, till all the birds of the wood flew away for fright; but the horse let him sing on, and made his way quietly over the fields to his master's house.

"Here he is, master," said he, "I have got the better of him:" and when the farmer saw his old servant, his heart relented, and he said. "Thou shalt stay in thy stable and be well taken care of." And so the poor old horse had plenty to eat, and lived — till he died.

JACOB AND WILHELM GRIMM

◀ *RIDING FREE*
BY HERMAN MARIL

ONCE UPON A TIME
WHEN THE
SUN SINKS LOW

Nighttime is also story time. Stories are how grown-ups prepare you for a good night's rest. Bedtime stories help you relax and that helps you to fall asleep.

Some of the best stories have helped put kids to sleep for many years. *Good Night Moon*, by Margaret Wise Brown, has been read as a bedtime story since 1947. Others, like *How Do Dinosaurs Say Goodnight*, by Jane Yolen, is not as old, but it still is a sleepy time favorite.

Some parents tell even older tales such as *Jack and the Beanstalk*, *Goldilocks and the Three Bears*, and *Sleeping Beauty*.

And often bedtime is when kids and their parents have time for a bedtime chat. You can talk about what happened during the day, about what was fun.

Some classic bedtime reading favorites:

- *Good Night Moon*
- *Green Eggs and Ham*
- *Little Bear* series
- *I Love You Through and Through*
- *Corduroy*
- *Earl the Squirrel*
- *What's Wrong Little Pookie*
- *If You Were Born a Kitten*
- *Peter and the Wolf*
- *Puff, the Magic Dragon*
- *Parts, More Parts, and Even More Parts*
- *No David* series
- *Fright Night Fright*
- *Mr. Brown Can Moo*
- *Time for Bed*
- *Snuggle Puppy*
- *The Polar Express*
- *Where the Wild Things Are*
- *Joss Bird*
- *Rootabaga Stories*
- *Hans Christian Andersen Fairy Tales and Stories*
- *Little House in the Big Woods*

The prince vowed to find his one true love at any cost.

Story Time

WHAT YOU NEED:
- TONS OF BOOKS
- SOFT LIGHTS
- FLASHLIGHT
- FAVORITE STUFFED ANIMALS
- CUDDLY BLANKETS

SKILLS:

 COLLABORATION

 CRITICAL THINKING

 COMMUNICATION

CREATIVE INNOVATION

CONTENT

Nighttime is the best time for snuggling up and telling stories. Here are some ideas to help you settle in for a good night's sleep.

1. Family Stories
Ask those who put you to bed to share a story about when they were little. What did they like to play? What was their favorite book? What were their parents like?

2. Share Your Day
On a scale of one to five how was your day? What did you do? Who did you play with? Did anything make you sad or scared? What made you laugh? And don't forget to ask your folks about their day, too. It is a nice way to end the day.

3. Sing a Song
Do you have a favorite song you like to sing every night? If not, why not make one up or find one you like. Some favorites include "Twinkle, Twinkle, Little Star" and James Taylor's "You Can Close Your Eyes."

4. Tongue Twisters and Nursery Rhymes
You know a million of them. Do you have a favorite?

5. Read a Poem
Poems are so perfect for bedtime because they put wonderful pictures in your head to dream about. There are many poems in this book!

6. Read a Book Out Loud
If you are old enough to read out loud, take turns with whoever is helping you go to bed.

Once Upon a time....

bathtime, bedtime, dreamtime

SNUGGLE BUNNY

Frère Jacques

Frère Jacques, Frère Jacques,
Dormez vous? Dormez vous?
Sonnez les matines,
Sonnez les matines.
Din don, don. Din, don, don.
Are you sleeping?
Are you sleeping?
Brother John, brother John?
Morning bells are ringing!
Morning bells are ringing!
Ding, dang, dong.
Ding, dang, dong.

FRENCH NURSERY SONG

Starlight, Star Bright

Starlight, star bright,
The first star
I see tonight,
I Wish I may,
I Wish I might,
Have this wish
I wish tonight.

**MOTHER GOOSE
NURSERY RHYME**

Sleeping Beauty

Twelve fairy godmothers blessed a baby princess. A grumpy thirteenth fairy had other ideas.

Beauty! Patience! Wisdom! The virtues went on and on as the first eleven fairies announced their blessings. And then the grumpy fairy appeared.
"The princess will die from the prick of a sewing needle!" she declared.

Everyone cried, but the smallest fairy spoke up. "Here is the very last blessing," she whispered. "The princess will not die, but sleep and awake only for courageous love."

To save the princess, sewing was outlawed. Yet when the princess was twelve, she found a spinning wheel and pricked her finger. At once, not only the princess but the whole kingdom fell under the spell of sleep for a hundred years, overgrown with thick vines and thorns.

Time after time, young men tried to prove true love by climbing through the vines. Finally, a prince had the courage to brave the forest and awaken the princess with a single kiss. She awoke with a smile and the thorny forest disappeared.

The twelve fairies appeared again to bless the prince and princess, and they all lived happily ever after.

FRENCH FAIRY TALE

◄ *GIRL WITH PUPPET HARE*
BY LARUS ALBENS

SNUGGLE BUNNY
NIGHT, SLEEP TIGHT

At bedtime, it's normal to feel nervous, because when you sleep in your own room, it's sometimes scary to spend the night away from your parents. It can be difficult for your parents, too, because they don't like the time away from you, either.

Moms and dads have a way to help both of you get through the night peacefully. They tuck you in, surrounding you snuggly in warm covers. And of course you have your favorite snuggle animal to wrap your arms around like a hug.

Some snuggle animals are bunnies, some teddy bears, some even dolphins. Most are soft and stuffed like a pillow and feel good against your skin. They help you relax and fall asleep.

Who is your snuggle friend?

Tucking in Your Snuggle Friends

WHAT YOU NEED:
- CUDDLY STUFFED FRIEND OR FRIENDS
- WARM BED

SKILLS:

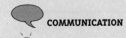 COMMUNICATION

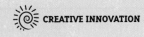 CREATIVE INNOVATION

CONTENT

After you have had your snack, brushed your teeth and gotten your pajamas on; after you have giggled and laughed and read out loud, there is nothing much left to do but snuggle in for a good night's sleep. Are you ready?

1. Off with your robe and slippers and climb into bed. Make sure you have your special cuddly stuffed friends close by your side.

2. Pull the covers up right under your buddies' chins and then your own.

3. Tell your cuddly friends a bedtime story or maybe something special about your day.

4. Make sure your buddies are cozy and warm.

5. Kiss your cuddly friends good night.

128 bathtime, bedtime, dreamtime

SWEET DREAMS

Sleep

And now 'tis Night, and with
　oblivious plume
Sleep fans the eyelids of the
　sons of care,
And souls to their mysterious
　haunts repair
Where the dim dreamland spread
　its warping gloom.
O sweet and soft the glories
　that illume
The land of dreams, and
　multiform as fair,
Brighter than gorgeous tissues
　of the loom,
Or sunset splendours of the
　waking air!
The worlding and his brother
　of the soil,
This one his toilsome, that his
　tedious day,
His suit the lawyer, and the
　smith his toil,
His rags the beggar, and the
　child its play-
Each his peculiar care forgets
　a while,
And all, sweet Sleep, under they
　peaceful sway.

JAMES L. ROBERTSON

Brahms Lullaby

Lullaby and good night;
With roses bedlight,
With lilies bested,
Is baby's wee bed.
Lay thee down now and rest,
May the slumber be blest.

Lullaby and good night,
Thy mother's delight;
Bright angels around
My darling shall stand;
They will guard thee from harm,
Thou shalt wake in my arms.

JOHANNES BRAHMS

Good Night

I love you
I love you,
I love you I do.
From the moment
I met you
I loved you I do.
You are my baby girl
　with the pretty blue eyes,
I love you, I love you I do.

AUTHOR UNKNOWN

◀ *COZY QUILT*
BY PAULA PERTILE

SWEET DREAMS
NIGHTY NIGHT

You sleep more than one-third of your life! Getting a good night's sleep is very important for your health.

The word "dream" comes from a Middle English word that meant "joy, mirth and musical sound." May your dreams be filled with joy!

Research studies show that our brains are very busy during dreaming and sleep.

All mammals need sleep. It helps you manage your mood and is very important for learning and memory.

Some studies suggest sleep is also critical in maintaining physical health, weight and more. Kids need between ten and twelve hours of sleep each night.

Time for bed!

Special Bedtime Rituals

WHAT YOU NEED:
- A TUCKERINER
- CUDDLY FRIENDS

SKILLS:
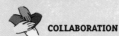 COLLABORATION 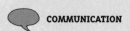 COMMUNICATION

Most families have special bedtime rituals, and you probably know yours by heart. But here are some from other families you could try.

1. Hugs and Kisses
Before you get completely under the blankets why not get, and give, the biggest hug in the history of the world? How tight can you squeeze? And what about those bedtime kisses? What is your record number for bedtime kisses?

2. Big Back Rub
There is nothing better than a gentle back rub to relax you. Lie on your stomach and let your tuckeriner quietly massage your back. Ahh, you are getting sleepy....

3. Glass of Water?
Is there anything else you need before the final stage of bedtime?

4. The Super Dooper Tuck In
Lie down in bed, face up, and get really comfortable. Make sure your cuddly friend is next to you. Now it is the tuckeriner's turn to make sure the blankets are situated around you just the way you like. The tuckeriner's job is to carefully tuck the blanket all around, making sure you are "snug as a bug in a rug." Caution: Tucking in is not the same as tickling!

5. Nightlights and Music
Don't forget to ask to have a nightlight and quiet music turned on before your tuckeriner leaves, if you would like.

6. And Last But Not Least...
Say "I love you" and listen for it back before you close your eyes and drift off to sleep.

See you in the morning!

SKILLS
THE 6 Cs™: DEVELOPING 21ST-CENTURY SKILLS

Kathy Hirsh-Pasek and Roberta M. Golinkoff, professors of child development, with the assistance of graduate student Jessa Reed, have created a developmental model that outlines six critical skills for children.

Throughout *The Classic Treasury of Childhood Wonders,* the 6 Cs™ have been used to provide a skills assessment and overview for each hands-on experience through a series of symbols at the top of each activity page. Parents and educators can use this simple guide to help reinforce essential skills.

The 6 C™ skills are Collaboration, Communication, Content, Critical thinking, Creative innovation and Confidence. The following provides an overview of the 6 Cs™.

1.  ## COLLABORATION

International collaboration and teamwork is the new reality. Schools, informal programs and curricula must encourage children to work together, to accommodate others' viewpoints and to circumvent one's weaknesses by calling upon the strengths of others. Collaboration includes building a sense of community, knowledge sharing, and co-constructing solutions toward a common goal. Collaboration is the foundational skill upon which all others build.

2.  ## COMMUNICATION

Collaboration allows for the flow of communication. Communication is the grease that enables international commerce to advance across geographic boundaries. Communication is about more than just form; it includes taking the listener's perspective, regardless of cultural differences, mastering rhetoric, and being a good listener not just a persuasive speaker.

3.  ## CONTENT

Until we have fluid communication, there is little opportunity to develop rich content. Children must engage with and master subject-matter content that is rich in depth and breadth. This includes mastery of reading and math, but goes beyond the 3R's to encompass science, art, and history.

4.  CRITICAL THINKING

With knowledge doubling every 2.5 years, just assembling content will not be enough. The cook with full cupboards still needs to find a good recipe. Twenty-first century workers must ask the right questions, find and synthesize necessary data and connect seemingly disparate facts. If knowledge is abundant, we must selectively attend to information that is important and evaluate the source of the information.

5.  CREATIVE INNOVATION

Even critical thinking will not be enough to succeed. In a world that is constantly changing we must be innovative, flexible, and adaptive. Future jobs will use our skills in ways that we cannot even imagine. Nurturing creative thinking is important for helping children become inventors, entrepreneurs, designers and more, building a productive global economy.

6.  CONFIDENCE

With content, critical thinking, and creativity in place, it is now time to take risks and develop the confidence to succeed — or to fail and try again.

6 Cs™ MASTERY LEVELS

	Level 1	Level 2	Level 3	Level 4
1. Collaboration	on my own	side by side	back and forth	building together
2. Communication	emotional expression	inform and tell	dialogue, broad breadth	tell a joint story
3. Content	narrow depth, narrow breadth	broad depth, narrow breadth	broad depth, broad breadth	expert
4. Critical Thinking	seeing is believing	truths differ	opinions	evidence
5. Creative Innovation	free flow	means-end	voice	vision
6. Confidence	barrel on	where do I stand	calculated risks	dare to fail

RESOURCES

OUTDOOR EXPLORING

IN THE GARDEN

Websites:
Filled with resources that teach gardening, an appreciation of nature, and making good food choices.
www.kidsgardening.com

The Youth Gardening Grants program: Children as young as three can apply for grants that have helped more than one million youngsters get involved in gardening.
www.kidsgardening.com/ygg.asp

Nature Explore: Created by the Arbor Day Foundation, Nature Explore is a research-based program that offers resources to help educators, families, and communities connect children with nature. www.arborday.org/explore/

Programs:
A Garden at Every School: A Rhode Island-based initiative that uses gardening as a means to develop children's self confidence and appreciation of nature.

SNOW, SNOW, SNOW

Book:
The Snowman Storybook, by Raymond Briggs: An award-winning book that tells the story of a young boy and a snowman going on a night of adventures.

DVD:
Frosty the Snowman: The 1969 holiday classic features arguably the most popular snowman ever, Frosty, who magically comes to life, delighting children and adults alike.

Website:
Includes such activities as Build a Snowman, which allows kids to make different types of snowmen by moving objects with the computer mouse. www.northpole.com

Online video:
How to Build a Snowman: Learn not only how to build a snowman, but also how to dress appropriately so you can stay warm. www.ehow.com

A SECRET PLACE

Books:
Secret Spaces of Childhood, by Elizabeth Goodenough: The book explores the many secret spaces envisioned by children. It also features stories from writers who talk about their secret places.

A Kids Guide to Building Forts, by Tom Birdseye: A book on how to build forts using everything from wood to discarded materials such as parts of an automobile.

Trees and Playhouses You Can Build, by David and Jeanie Stiles: Transform your backyard into a place of wonder. The book shows how to make all types of tree houses.

DVD:
Shalom Sesame: Journey to Secret Places: Part of a Sesame Street education series that journeys through Israel.

SALT, SEA & SAND

CD:
Under the Mystic Sea, by Maria Sangiolo: Delightful collection of children's songs about underwater adventures.

Events:
Swimming with the Sharks at The National Aquarium in Baltimore: Do a sleepover with a group of friends or classmates at the National Aquarium.

The South Padre Island Sand Castle Competition: About two dozen of the world's most prolific sand castle builders converge on this Texas shoreline town for this annual fun-filled meet. www.sandcastledays.com

DVD:
The Riddle in a Bottle: Solve riddles while learning about underwater animals, tides, and weather.

RUN AND PLAY

Book:
Brainiac's Secret Agent Activity Book: *Fun Activities for Spies of All Ages*, by Sarah Jane Prian: Here's a chance to become a spy.

Websites:
Today Is Fun: The site encourages families to conjure up unique and exciting ways to have fun without making trips to the department store. It makes use of everyday household items. www.todayisfun.com/blog

Origami For Kids: Parents can work with kids in learning how to fold paper into many different objects for show or play.
www.origami-instructions.com/origami-for-kids.html

Hand Clapping Games: Remember the hand clapping game, Miss Mary Mack? This site offers the words to that and other timeless hand clapping games.
www.childstoryhour.com/gamesclapping.htm

ENCHANTED NIGHTS

Book:
Fireflies, by Julie Brinckloe: The story of a boy who catches fireflies then discovers they must be set free.

Websites:
This site offers facts about fireflies (they emit light mostly to attract mates, but also to defend their territory), the different types of fireflies, and how to catch fireflies. www.firefly.org

The site explains the best way to attract fireflies to your backyard. It encourages families to cut down on the use of pesticides and eliminate as much artificial light as possible. www.backyardwildlifehabitat.intro/fireflies.htm

WIND AT MY BACK

Books:
Klutz Book of Paper Airplanes, by Doug Stillinger: Do not let the title fool you. This book offers ways to make any novice a top-shelf paper airplane builder.

The World Paper Airplane Book, by Jeff Lammers and Ken Black-burn: The book takes paper airplane building to new heights. Co-written by Blackburn, the paper airplane expert who set distance records with his planes.

WANDERING & WONDERING

Books:
Nature's Playground: Activities, Crafts and Games to Encourage Children to Get Outdoors, by Fiona Danks and Jo Schofield: Play outdoor games, probe the lives of animals and insects, collect seashells.

Why Do Leaves Change Color, by Betsy Maestro: a look at the transformation that leaves go through during autumn.

Websites:
Creative Backyard Camping: Pitch a tent. Build a small fire. Toast some marshmallows. All within the confines of your backyard. http://www.homemadesimple.com/en_US/nbr-content.do?contentType=op&articleId=ar003

Outdoor Games: Red Light, Green Light. Simon Says. Hide and Seek. This site conjures up some of the more popular outdoor games, as well as a few many may not have heard mentioned in years.
www.indianchild.com/outdoor_games.htm

PLAY BALL!

Websites:
Youth Baseball Skills and Drills for Free: Learn hitting, pitching, fielding, catching, base running and more. www.weplay.com/youth-baseball/drills

Take Me Out To the Ball Game: Learn about the 1908 Jack Norworth classic song that's sung at ball parks throughout the country. www.baseball-almanac.com/poetry/po_stmo.shtml

DVD:
How to Play Basketball: An instructional video that teaches the fundamentals of the game, from beginner to advanced.

DREAM IT MAKE IT
CATCHING YOUR SHADOW

Website:
"The Shadow Radio Show": Download podcasts of the once-popular radio show "The Shadow." The Shadow began as a narrator for other popular detective shows. www.oldtimeradiofans.com/template.php.show_name=The%20Shadow

STORIES COME TO LIFE

Events:
The National Storytelling Festival: What began in 1973 with a teacher and his class in Jonesborough, Tenn., has become one of the most popular events for storytelling in the country.

DVD:
The Scholastic Video Collection: A 27-volume set of mostly animated adaptations of some of the most renowned children's books.

HAND IN HAND

Books:
Hands Around the World: 365 Creative Ways to Encourage Cultural Awareness and Global Respect, by Susan Milford. With each day of the year, children learn a delightful new way to appreciate diversity and respect for others.

The Lion and the Mouse: The ferocious lion spares the mouse's life, unaware that one day the feeble animal will end up returning the favor.

Websites:
Teaching Kids Business: A program that helps kids participate in community service initiatives. www.teachingkidsbusiness.com

Children Involved in Community Service: A website filled with projects, programs, and resources that help encourage kids to volunteer and make a difference. www.artistshelpingchildren.org

EVERYDAY ART

Website:
Author Susan Taylor Brown shows kids how to make log cabins from cardboard tube rolls and ring toss games from plastic coffee can lids. www.susantaylorbrown.com

Movie:
Batteries Not Included: A science fiction film about extraterrestrial beings that fix up old appliances and transform scraps into workable devices.

DVD:
The Magic School Bus Holiday Special, Recycling: En route to see a showing of the Nutcracker, a little girl's toy soldier is destroyed in a recycling bin. She blames the recycling process for destroying her treasured toy but is given a valuable lesson in the importance of recycling.

FROM THE EARTH

Books:
The Kids 'N' Clay Ceramics Book, by Kevin Nierman and Elaine Arima: Shows kids how to make all types of ceramic projects.

Fun With Modeling Clay, by Barbara Reid: For grades 1-4. Kids can learn to roll clay into balls and snakes then move on to create bugs, birds, cats and more.

Museum:
The Uhrichsville Clay Museum in Uhrichsville, Ohio, features the clay making history of an area once hailed as the clay capital of the world, with more than 30 clay manufacturing plants.

DVD:
Gumby: One of the oldest and most popular clay-made characters in animation history. Features a green clay boy named Gumby and his sidekick animal, Pokey.

MAGIC AND MAKE-BELIEVE
ANYTHING'S POSSIBLE

Books:
The Tall Book of Make-Believe, by Jane Werner: First published in 1950, the book is a collection of some of the most popular make-believe stories.

Where the Wild Things Are, by Maurice Sendak: The timeless adventure tale of what can happen to a feisty little boy who is sent to bed with no supper. Also now adapted to a motion picture, but arguably the book is better.

Harold and the Purple Crayon, by Crockett Johnson: An unassuming boy doubles as sketch artist, using a long, purple crayon to conjure up some of the most imaginative places and things.

Movie:
Alice in Wonderland: A remake of the timeless classic tale; a teenaged Alice returns to the fantasy world from her childhood.

DREAM A LITTLE DREAM

Website:
Child Dream Interpreter: It lists, in alphabetical order, everything from animals to plants to objects to actions and emotions, and explains what each means to a dreaming child. http://dream.kaboose.com/symbols

DVD:
The Wizard of Oz: Adapted from a children's novel, the 1939 fantasy film features one of the most infamous dreams ever, that of a little girl who during a violent tornado is knocked unconscious, then dreams of being whisked away to a wonderfully magical, but sometimes scary, faraway place.

CD:
Indigo Ocean Dreams: Relaxation and Meditation. Stories for children, improve sleep, manage stress and anxiety. Fun, interactive stories that help kids sleep.

Dream Child: A Children's Relaxation CD: Filled with music that helps kids sleep, it also includes relaxation techniques, magical stories and uplifting songs.

FAIRY MAGIC

Books:
The Fairy House Series, by Tracy Kane: It is the story of a little girl who makes a miniature home for fairies among a village of other little houses, only to have it visited by real fairies.

The Red Fairy Book, by Andrew Lang: The book consists of more than three dozen fairy tales from all over the world.

DVDs:
Peter Pan: The Disney-animated film features the fairy Tinker Bell, a feisty yet helpful fairy with glistening wings and a leafy green dress.

Fairy Tale: A True Story: Two girls discover fairies in a garden and photograph them. That's where the fun really begins.

MEDIEVAL QUEST

Books:
The Book of the Dragon, by H. Gustavo Ciruelo Cabral: The author brings the magical world of the flying, fire-breathing creatures to life, with colorful, adventurous stories about different types of dragons.

Dragon Art, by Jessica Peffer: Not only learn about dragons but also learn how to draw them with step-by-step instructions, and accompany them with drawings of gargoyles and other creatures.

Website:
Dragons in art and on the web: The site contains more than 1,500 resources about dragons, as well as more than 1,000 photos and more than 400 links to other dragon sites. www.isidore-of-seville.com/dragons

Event:
Medieval Times: In various locations throughout the U.S.; take a journey back to the age of knights and epic battles, jousting tournaments and royal feasts.

BE A SUPERHERO

Books, Movies and Comics:
Superman: The DC comics flagship character, the most legendary hero of all, and the standard by which all superheroes are measured.

The Superhero Book, by Gina Misiroglu: All of your favorites are here. The author offers information on more than 300 heroes, villains and comic characters.

DVDs:
The Incredibles: A family of superheroes tries to live a quiet comfortable life in the suburbs before being called upon to wage one more battle against the forces of evil.

Last Action Hero: A fantasy comedy about a fictional Los Angeles crime fighter and a young boy who enjoys watching his films. While watching one of the films, the boy is suddenly transported into the make-believe world.

CLANG, CLANG, BANG, BANG

Website:
Musical Instrument Crafts for Kids: Learn to make drums of all shapes and sizes. www.artistshelpingchildren.org/musicalinstrumentsartscraftstideashandmadekids.html

Show:
Stomp: A one-of-a-kind percussion show where performers demonstrate pulsating beats by banging on everything from garbage can lids to kitchen pots and pans. www.stomponline.com

Event:
The World Music Drum Festival: Part of the annual Virginia Arts Festival, it includes youth drummers from around the world.

LET'S PUT ON A SHOW

Book:
On Stage, Theater Games and Activities for Kids, by Lisa Bany Winters: The book includes such games as Mirrors and Freeze and teaches kids about makeup, costumes and puppetry.

Websites:
ArtReach Children's Theatre Plays: The group is known for crafting award-winning plays for children. www.artreachchildrenstheatreplays.com

Creative Drama and Resource Site: Offers different types of games, typically used in a theater classroom, that can influence performance and creative skills. www.creativedrama.com/theatre.htm

Pioneer Drama Service, Inc.: Teaches youngsters all aspects of the stage with a collection of theater games. There are ensemble building games, vocal games, exercises in mask making, puppetry and set designs. www.pioneerdrama.com/searchdetail.asp?pc=ONSTAGEKID

SILLY TIME

Book:
Silly Sports and Goofy Games, by Spencer Kagan: These games are designed to get kids off their seats and involved in high-energy action, for both indoors and outdoors.

Websites:
Fun and Silly Games: From puzzle games (Magic Balls, Bejeweled, Bookworm) to action games (Panik, Bug on a Wire, Sheepish) to sports games (Mini Pool, Surfs Up, Super Bike), many of the more popular fun and silly games are here. www.funsilly.com/free-online-games

Funny Games: One of the largest selection of games that any site has to offer, including arcade games, puzzle games, board games, sport games and muli-player games. www.funny-games.biz/main.html

YUMMY IN MY TUMMY

Book:

The Kids-Did-It! Cookie Bookie: A cookie-baking cookbook for kids, illustrated by kids.

Websites:

Homemade Soup Recipes: Includes chicken noodle, navy bean, cheesy broccoli and split pea.
http://oldrecipebook.com/easysouprecipes.shtml

Sandwich recipes: A site that boasts it has the world's largest collection of sandwich recipes.
www.sandwichrecipes.org/

Ice Cream Making for Kids: Offers ways to make ice cream in plastic bags, in coffee cans and from snow.
www.makeicecream.com/icecreammakf.html

Cookie Recipes for Kids: Includes no-bake chocolate cookies, red velvet cookies, and peanut butter and jelly bars.
http://allhomemadecookies.com/recipeindex/kidsrecipes.htm

Event:

The Great American Pie Festival: The annual event in Celebration, Fla., features an enormous pie buffet, ice cream, and beverages.

Venues:

The World's Longest Candy Counter: The store in Littleton, NH, has set the Guinness World Record for the longest candy store counter.

Hershey Park in Hershey, Pa.: More than 60 rides. Family entertainment. Bands. Concerts. Holiday events. And lots of chocolate.

BATHTIME, BEDTIME, DREAMTIME

RUB, A DUB, DUB

Toys:

Boon Scrubble Interchangeable Bath Toy Scrub Set: Helps get the body clean by making scrubbing in the tub fun.

Tub Tunes Water Flutes by Alex Toys: Make real sounds with the water-safe flutes. Fill the flutes with water for different sounds.

Device:

MP3 Bath Speaker, by Pomme: Plug in your music device and allow kids to listen to their favorite music while in the bath. Surrounds any room with stereo sound.

SWEET DREAMS

Books:

The Golden Book of Fairy Tales, by Marie Ponsot: No children's home library is complete without it.

Favorite Nursery Rhymes from Mother Goose, by Scott Gustafson. Relive the classic rhyming tales from childhood days while kids learn them.

Goodnight Moon, by Margaret Wise Brown. The consummate bedtime book.

Website:

Grimm Fairy Tales: Animated versions of some of the most beloved children's fairy tales and folk stories.
www.grimmfairytales.com/ren/main

CDs:

Putumayo Kids African Dreamland, by Various Artists: Various artists from Africa come together to make two hours of soothing music that helps children fall to sleep.

The Ultimate Lullaby Collection: Includes "Twinkle, Twinkle, Little Star," "Brahms Lullaby" and "Rock-A-Bye Baby." Enough said.

INDEX

AFTERWORD

People often ask me, "How long have you been working on this book?" Usually I say it has been two years in development, but the truth is, I have been working on *The Classic Treasury of Childhood Wonders* my entire life! It represents so much of my own childhood, my beliefs as a parent and as an educator and advocate for families. And I have loved every single moment I have worked on this rare and precious project. I hope *Childhood Wonders* will find a place on many families' bookshelves and in their hearts for years to come.

This book was mostly researched and written in the blizzards of 2009 and 2010. With more than 30 inches of snow, our family settled in with a warm fire, lots of hot chocolate, soothing music and timelessness—a rare commodity. We were snowbound for over a week, newfound time to think, nap, dream, and write. I can think of no better gift than this to write about childhood wonders. We wandered, took walks, cooked comfort food, and had a lot of fun. This special time that was created to write this book is symbolic of my aspiration for *Childhood Wonders*—uninterrupted time to enjoy family, share adventures, and create something new.

Childhood Wonders, like all of my work, is one big collaborative project. It started with the National Geographic Society staff, which has been an extraordinary partner. We began dreaming about developing a special book for families with young children over two years ago. There are no words to express my gratitude or fondness for each of these colleagues, but I mention them here if only to be sure these pages will forever hold my eternal thanks. Nina Hoffman, Executive Vice President and President of the Book Publishing Group, has been a longtime friend and supporter of hands-on exploration and learning. Melina Gerosa Bellows, Executive Vice President, Children's Publishing, saw the need for an instant classic and simply made it happen with style and smarts. Nancy Feresten, Vice President and Editor-in-Chief, National Geographic Children's Books, a fellow traveler, is always willing to listen to a new idea, talk it through and create something different. Jennifer Emmett, Executive Editor, Reference and Solo, Children's Books, delights and amazes me with her kindness, thoughtfulness, and savvy about children's publishing. Jonathan Halling, Design Director, Children's Publishing, worked to get the design grid just right from the start and carefully thought about each creative decision along the way. Lori Epstein, Illustrations Editor, Children's Books, did a remarkable job of finding photographs and art. Kate Olesin, Editorial Assistant, helped to keep everyone on track. Linda Howey, Vice President and Director, Retail Sales, made sure we created a book that would stand the test of time and find a home in bookstores. Bill O'Donnell, Director of Retail and Special Sales, worked to find innovative sales channels to broaden the reach of *Childhood Wonders*. The entire sales and marketing team at NGS, too many to name, the folks at Random House and more are among the most creative and productive teams I have ever worked with.

It has also been a delight to put together a creative team under the SharingStories umbrella to develop *Childhood Wonders*. The original design template for this book was developed by Lotta Olen, a longtime collaborator. Research and editorial support contributors included Nina Kamooei, Joe Burris and Ellen Wilson. Cathy Evans, owner of Shoot the Moon, completed the design and production of the book with grace and magic. Kathryn Goldman managed all rights and releases and legal issues. She literally saved me on every page and made me follow the rules. Debbie Haer worked as our editor and fact checker. Her careful attention to every detail is greatly appreciated, as is her appreciation for the need for a book like this one. Connie Binder developed the index for *Childhood Wonders*. I am in awe of how she can take so much information and organize it so beautifully, making it easy to find anything. Googie Goldman has been a calm voice whispering in my ear, helping me remember the important things in life. Each person on the team brought a unique talent and insight to this project and collectively conspired to creative something rare and special.

The artwork throughout *Childhood Wonders* will take your breath away. Many of these images have memories attached to my childhood like "Riding Free," by Herman Maril, or "Little Monkey," created by my sister Sandra Magsamen. "Jennie Penny," the very, very talented illustrator whose work is represented throughout this book, shines brightly. I am sure she is destined to be among the most gifted children's book illustrators. Thank you, Jennie, for your amazing talent and also for your ability to listen carefully and let your imagination go wild. Your work has made this an even more special book. To see more of her work go to www. jenniepenny.com. Chris Sheban is the illustrator that created the cover illustration. I have admired Chris's work for years and it is a thrill to work with him. His work is magical and timeless. Thank you for letting me enter your wonderful, creative world. To enjoy more of Chris's work visit www.chrissheban.com.

The art selections were chosen to share with families a range of styles, periods and topics. Special thanks must be given to the following people that helped to bring beautiful art to this book. Marcia Weber, owner of Art Objects in Montgomery, Alabama, represents visionary artists, several of which are represented in *Childhood Wonders*, including Woodie Long, Bernice Sims, and Della Wells. What makes these artists' work unique is that they are untrained. Many paint, create and draw because it is the best way for them to express themselves. This form of art feels so right for this book. Last year, Woodie Long passed away, so it is with great pride we include his work with permission from his wife, Dot Long.

The literature selections in *Childhood Wonders* are vast, aspiring to offer something from the rich collection of children's stories, songs, nursery rhymes, poetry and sayings. Thank you to all who have allowed me to include your work. To families, foundations, trusts of work, I too appreciate your good will. I am indebted to Navajo poet John Hershman for allowing the use of "Four Breaths," which first appeared in 2005 in the literary magazine *Puerto del Sol*. Thank you to Jane Yolen. You are simply the most amazing author. There is one entry that is very special to me above all. It is by my son, Ben Garrett, on page 33, entitled "Take the Back Roads." This poem was written in honor of his running coach and teacher, Tony Smith, who died suddenly several years ago. Tony, his family and friends have been a constant inspiration to our family—reminding us that life is short and we need to embrace and celebrate one another every moment.

Childhood Wonders incorporates a new level of developmental psychology and child development, offering families and teachers practical and reliable ways to use the activities in this book to introduce and reinforce learning and skills. I am very proud to have had wonderful advisors to inform and inspire this work. Dr. Kathy Hirsh-Pasek and Dr. Roberta Golinkoff, who developed the 6 Cs™ and are authors of *A Mandate for Playful Learning in Preschool*, generously shared their thinking and work. Thanks, too, to Jessa Reed, a graduate student who helped develop the 6 Cs™. Ellen Galinsky, Co-Founder of Families and Work Institute and author of *Mind in the Making*, has been a constant go-to friend and colleague. Dr. Mariale Hardiman, Co-Director of the Neuro-Education Initiative at the Johns Hopkins University School of Education and author of *Connecting Brain Research with Effective Teaching: The Brain-Targeted Teaching Model*, has been a wonderful collaborator and inspiration in validating the role arts-integration can play. Dr. Kurt Fischer, Scholar in Residence, Ross School, Charles Warland Bigelow Professor, Director of Mind, Brain, and Education Program at Harvard Graduate School of Education, has taught me so much about the marriage of the arts and sciences and the power to transform lives with this knowledge. And finally, a special thanks to my dear friend Alice Wilder, educational psychologist and creator and collaborator of Think It Ink It Publishing, "Super Why," Kidos and "Blue's Clues." I love how you think!

The FamilyStories model of collecting ideas and stories was used to put this book together. *The Classic Treasury of Childhood Wonders* would not have been possible without the hundreds of contributions made to the book by families, educators, counselors, therapists and more. Through FamilyStories.org, people are invited to share their stories about moments that matter in their lives, and to listen and learn from other families. FamilyStories also gathers stories from a variety of venues, including our website, workshops, family reunions and get-togethers, personal interviews, festivals and any other places families meet.

Thanks to the good nature and creative spirit of Joe Schumacher, President and CEO of the Goddard Schools, *Childhood Wonders* was able to partner with affiliated parents, teachers and owners. A special thanks must go out to the "girls club"—Lee Scott, Sue Adair, Lisa Fisher and Robin Leon—for all of the great brainstorming, organizing and communicating. I want to thank The Goddard Schools for playing an integral role in developing the look, feel and content for this book. Goddard was selected to help us in the book's creation because of its commitment to providing the best in early childhood education through playful learning.

My longtime colleagues Mary Bonner and Lisa Hamm did not go on this journey with me, as they have done so many times in the past, but I need to thank them nonetheless. Often throughout this process I would find myself asking "What would Lisa and Mary do here?" Somehow they spoke to me and I moved on. A book like *Childhood Wonders* is filled with a million decisions and details, and it takes on a life of its own. It also has great power to evoke memories, thoughts, hopes and aspirations. Throughout this process I was reminded of things I did with my sisters growing up, how grateful I am for parents who thought anything was possible, and for grandparents who loved to play. I can now see more clearly than ever that how I played as a child has helped to shape the person I have become and the kind of parent I am.

And finally to my kind and generous family—Rick, Ben, Sam, Nikki and Adam—thank you for loving how much I have loved the adventure of this book. And thank you for indulging me in so many rambling stories that have no endings.

Literature Credits

13, "Tree Fort," Richard L. Provencher
59, "Four Breaths." Puerto del Sol. Las Cruces: New Mexico State University Press, Summer/Fall 2005.
77, "Why Dragons?" Copyright © 1993 by Jane Yolen. First appeared in *Here There Be Dragons*, published by Harcourt Brace and Company. Reprinted by permission of Curtis Brown, Ltd.
117, "My Tub," Copyright © 1987, Kathy Hirsh-Pasek and Monica Goldman Zakhem

Illustration Credits

All line illustrations by Jennie Penny.

FRONT MATTER
Cover & Endpapers: Chris Sheban; Title Page, Comstock Select/ Corbis; Foreword, James M. Gurney/ NationalGeographicStock.com;

2-3, Martin Ruegner/ Photographer's Choice RF/ Getty Images. Back cover: istockphoto.com

OUTDOOR EXPLORING
4, Sargent, John Singer (1856-1925). *Carnation, Lily, Lily, Rose*, 1885-86. Oil on canvas. Photo Credit: Tate, London/ Art Resource, NY; 8, Bergander, Rudolf (1909-1970). *Snowball Fight.* 1960. Oil on canvas. Photo Credit: 2010 Artists Rights Society (ARS), New York/VG Bild-Kunst, Bonn; 12, Nomeko/ Shutterstock; 16, Potthast, Edward Henry (1857-1927). *Ring around the Rosy*, c. 1915. Oil on panel. Daniel J. Terra Collection. Photo Credit: Terra Foundation for American Art, Chicago/ Art Resource, NY; 20, *Little Monkey* by Sandra Magsamen/ Sandra Magsamen Permission; 24, The Palma Collection/ Stockbyte/ Getty Images; 28, *Yellow Jacket* by Colleen M. Madden/ MB Artists; 31, *The Secret*

Zoo by Chris Sheban with permission from Brian Chick; 36, *Baseball* by Mackey Pamintuan/ MB Artists

DREAM IT, MAKE IT
40-41, Nigel Pavitt / awl-images; 42, Macara, Andrew (Contemporary Artist). *Footballers, KOS.* Oil on canvas. Photo credit: Private Collection/ The Bridgeman Art Library/ Getty Images; 46, Puller, John Anthony (1821-67). *Punch and Judy.* Oil on panel. Photo Credit: Haynes Fine Art at the Bindery Galleries, Broadway/ The Bridgeman Art Library/ Getty Images; 50, *Nothing But Miracles* by Susan L. Roth; 54, *Don't Forget to Wash My Blanket* by Della Wells/ Art Objects; 58, *Little American Beauty* by Jean Hildebrant/ Jean Hildebrant Permission

MAGIC AND MAKE-BELIEVE
62-63, Jennifer Short/ jenniferbshort.com; 64, *The Little Explorer* by Elizabeth Sayles/

Elizabeth Sayles Permission; 68, Wyeth, N.C. (1882-1945). *The Giant* (1923). Oil on canvas. Collection of Westtown School, Westtown, PA. Photograph courtesy of The Brandywine River Museum; 72, Hughes, Edward Robert (1851-1914). *Midsummer Eve.* Watercolor. Photo Credit: © The Maas Gallery, London, UK/ The Bridgeman Art Library/ Getty Images; 76, *Dragon and Boy* by Kathi Ember/ MB Artists; 80, Mark Murphy/ iStockphoto.com; 84, *New Orleans Jazz Musicians* by Woodie Long/ Art Objects; 88, Ditz (Contemporary Artist). *Private View.* Photo Credit: Ditz/ Private Collection/ The Bridgeman Art Library/ Getty Images; 92, *Children Dancing with Animals* by Valerie Cis/ MB Artists

YUMMY IN MY TUMMY
96-97 Melanie Acevedo/ Botanica/ Getty

Images (digitally altered); 98, *Thanksgiving Dinner* by Bernice Sims/ Art Objects; 102, Bogaevsky, Konstantin Fedorovich (1872-1943). *The Birthday.* Oil on canvas. Photo Credit: State Russian Museum, St. Petersburg, Russia/ Giraudon/ The Bridgeman Art Library/ Getty Images; 106, *Baking* by Valeria DoCampo/ MB Artists; 110, Hyacinth Manning (b.1954/American). *Sunday Morning,* Oil on canvas. Photo Credit: Private Collection/ Getty Images

BATHTIME, BEDTIME, DREAMTIME
114-115, Theo Westenberger/ NationalGeographicStock.com; 116, Bathtub by Kathi Ember/ MB Artists; 120, *Riding Free* by Herman Maril with permission from David Maril; 124, Larus Albens/ Shutterstock; 128, *Cozy Quilt* by Paula Pertile/ Paula Pertile Permission

To my husband, and our wild and beautiful family—S.H.M.

BIOGRAPHY
SUSAN H. MAGSAMEN

Susan is an award-winning writer, educator and advocate on family and children's issues. Her books and programs have been called "a beautiful celebration of family life," empowering parents and children to connect—with each other, with other families and with the world around them. Susan's work is widely recognized as fostering and enhancing the ways we learn, play, create, and grow as individuals, families and communities.

Susan is the Founder of FamilyStories, a resource for families featuring a five-part book series, workshops, website and radio programs; Creator of Curiosityville, an on-and-off line learning world under development; Co-Director of the The Johns Hopkins University School of Education Neuro-Education Initiative, fostering dialogue, research and communications among educators, researchers and key stakeholders; Co-Director of CIRCLE (Center For Reimaging Children's Lives) at Temple University, where she is collaborating on a new family outreach initiative called The Ultimate Block Party; and Founder of Curiosity Kits, a hands-on learning company in the arts, sciences and world cultures. Susan is also a board member of the American Visionary Art Museum and served as Chair of the Editorial Advisory Council for *Wondertime Magazine*, an award-winning monthly publication on child development for families.

Susan has developed successful family, parent, children and school partnerships and collaborations with a variety of organizations including Johns Hopkins University, Temple University, Barnes & Noble, United Way of America, XM Radio, Goddard Schools, Scholastic Inc., National Geographic Society, Sylvan Learning Systems, Public Broadcasting Company, Discovery Channel, Metropolitan Museum of Art, Smithsonian Institutions, American Visionary Art Museum, Chicago Art Institute and The Walt Disney Company.

Her body of work has earned hundreds of national awards and recognition from child development experts and parenting associations including Oppenheim Awards, Parents' Choice, Family Fun, National Association of Parenting Publications Awards, Hearthsong and the prestigious Canadian Toy Council Award. To learn more visit www.familystories.org.

Recent Publications:
- *10 Best of Everything: Families*
- *Learning, Arts and the Brain*
- *FamilyStories: My Two Homes*
- *FamilyStories: Nighty Night*
- *FamilyStories: Tooth Fairy Time*
- *FamilyStories: Making Spirits Bright*
- *FamilyStories: Family Night!*

Published by the National Geographic Society

John M. Fahey, Jr., *President and Chief Executive Officer*

Gilbert M. Grosvenor, *Chairman of the Board*

Tim T. Kelly, President, *Global Media Group*

John Q. Griffin, *Executive Vice President; President, Publishing*

Nina D. Hoffman, *Executive Vice President; President, Book Publishing Group*

Melina Gerosa Bellows, *Executive Vice President, Children's Publishing*

Prepared by the Book Division

Nancy Laties Feresten, *Vice President, Editor in Chief, Children's Books*

Jonathan Halling, *Design Director, Children's Publishing*

Jennifer Emmett, *Executive Editor, Reference and Solo, Children's Books*

Carl Mehler, *Director of Maps*

R. Gary Colbert, *Production Director*

Jennifer A. Thornton, *Managing Editor*

Staff for This Book

Jennifer Emmett, *Project Editor*

Lori Epstein, *Illustrations Editor*

Priyanka Lamichhane, *Associate Editor*

Kate Olesin, *Editorial Assistant*

Grace Hill, *Associate Managing Editor*

Lewis R. Bassford, *Production Manager*

Susan Borke, *Legal and Business Affairs*

Manufacturing and Quality Management

Christopher A. Liedel, *Chief Financial Officer*

Phillip L. Schlosser, *Vice President*

Chris Brown, *Technical Director*

Nicole Elliott, *Manager*

Rachel Faulise, *Manager*

The National Geographic Society is one of the world's largest nonprofit scientific and educational organizations. Founded in 1888 to "increase and diffuse geographic knowledge," the Society works to inspire people to care about the planet. National Geographic reflects the world through its magazines, television programs, films, music and radio, books, DVDs, maps, exhibitions, live events, school publishing programs, interactive media and merchandise. *National Geographic* magazine, the Society's official journal, published in English and 32 local-language editions, is read by more than 35 million people each month. The National Geographic Channel reaches 310 million households in 34 languages in 165 countries. National Geographic Digital Media receives more than 13 million visitors a month. National Geographic has funded more than 9,200 scientific research, conservation and exploration projects and supports an education program promoting geography literacy. For more information, visit nationalgeographic.com.

For more information, please call 1-800-NGS LINE (647-5463) or write to the following address:
National Geographic Society
1145 17th Street N.W.
Washington, D.C. 20036-4688 U.S.A.

Visit us online at www.nationalgeographic.com/books

For librarians and teachers: www.ngchildrensbooks.org

More for kids from National Geographic:
kids.nationalgeographic.com

For information about special discounts for bulk purchases, please contact National Geographic Books Special Sales: ngspecsales@ngs.org

For rights or permissions inquiries, please contact National Geographic Books Subsidiary Rights: ngbookrights@ngs.org

BAL edition ISBN: 978-1-4263-0982-3
Trade hardcover ISBN: 978-1-4263-0715-7
Library edition ISBN: 978-1-4263-0726-3

Printed in the United States of America
11/WOR/1 (BAL edition)